M000086644

Less Is More in Elementary School

In this era of rigorous standards, testing, and overcrowded curricula, many teachers are left wondering how they're ever going to cover the material. *Less Is More in Elementary School* offers realistic solutions by providing ways teachers can streamline their curriculum, get the most out of assessment, communicate with families, and engage students in their own learning. This much-needed book will help you meet the demands of the Common Core more efficiently and effectively.

You'll learn how to . . .

- integrate the curriculum so that you can take time to slow down and explore topics in depth;
- help students become critical readers, problem solvers, collaborators, and communicators;
- make students more engaged, reflective, and self-regulating;
- get the most out of assessment during this era of high-stakes testing;
- maintain high expectations for all students but modify instruction to ensure all students progress;
- communicate more effectively with families to build trust during a time of change and high-stakes assessments; and
- overcome obstacles, such as the emphasis on testing, the need for more technology, and finding teacher collaboration time.

Each chapter is filled with practical strategies that you can implement immediately, as well as suggested resources for learning more about a particular topic.

Renee Rubin is an educational consultant specializing in literacy, ELLs, and family engagement. Previously, she taught elementary schools for 11 years and taught pre-service and in-service teachers at the University of Texas at Brownsville for 13 years.

Michelle H. Abrego is an associate professor at the University of Texas at Brownsville in the educational leadership program where she prepares principals and superintendents.

John A. Sutterby is an associate professor at the University of Texas at San Antonio in the area of early childhood education.

Flipping Your English Class to Reach All Learners:
Strategies and Lesson Plans
Troy Cockrum

Inquiry and Innovation in the Classroom:
Using 20% Time, Genius Hour, and PBL to Drive
Student Success
AJ Juliani

Using Children's Literature to Teach Problem
Solving in Math:
Addressing the Common Core in K-2
Jeanne White

Less Is More in Elementary School

Strategies for Thriving in a High-Stakes Environment

Renee Rubin, Michelle H. Abrego, and
John A. Sutterby

Routledge
Taylor & Francis Group

NEW YORK AND LONDON

First published 2015
by Routledge
711 Third Avenue, New York, NY 10017

and by Routledge
2 Park Square, Milton Park, Abingdon, Oxon, OX14 4RN

*Routledge is an imprint of the Taylor & Francis Group,
an informa business*

Library of Congress Cataloging-in-Publication Data
Rubin, Renee, 1954–
    Less is more in elementary school : strategies for thriving in
a high-stakes environment / Renee Rubin, Michelle Abrego,
John Sutterby.
        pages cm
    Includes bibliographical references.
    1. Elementary school teaching. 2. Effective teaching.
    3. Education, Elementary—Curricula. I. Abrego, Michelle H.
    II. Sutterby, John A., 1966– III. Title.
    LB1555.R83 2014
    372.1102—dc23
    2014016460

ISBN: 978-1-138-02230-0 (hbk)
ISBN: 978-1-138-02231-7 (pbk)
ISBN: 978-1-315-77710-8 (ebk)

Typeset in Palatino
by Apex CoVantage, LLC

Contents

Acknowledgments

Less Is More in Elementary School was written from the ideas and inspiration of many people, far too numerous to name here. However, the authors would like to give special thanks to those who took time to answer our questions and offer their expertise during the writing of this book.

We acknowledge Jesus "Chuey" Abrego for his keen feedback on the implementation of Professional Learning Communities, Kathy Bussert-Webb for reminding us that multiple modalities are essential to reach all learners, Allan Delesantro for his advice concerning the cover design, Caryl Lee Fisher for her guidance in crafting the text, Alex Garcia for explaining the realities of technology in the schools. Bobbette Morgan for practicing and clarifying student and adult collaborative work, and Paula Parson for providing thoughtful feedback on the critical readers and communicators chapters.

Meet the Authors

Renee Rubin is an educational consultant, specializing in literacy, English language learners, and family engagement. Previously, she taught elementary school for 11 years in New Mexico and Texas. She also taught courses on how to enhance elementary school students' literacy skills at the University of Texas at Brownsville. Her pre-service and in-service teachers often felt overwhelmed by the overcrowded curriculum and high-stakes testing.

Michelle H. Abrego is an associate professor at the University of Texas at Brownsville. Her research interests include administrative support for novice teachers, aspiring principal and pre-service teacher preparation, and family involvement. She has prior experience as a teacher, school leader, regional service center specialist, and program director at a state educational agency.

John A. Sutterby is an associate professor at the University of Texas San Antonio. His research interests include children's play and play culture, professional development of early childhood educators, and family involvement. His teaching experience was in pre-kindergarten in second language contexts.

The three authors previously wrote *Engaging the Families of ELLs: Ideas Resources, and Activities* (2012). Larchmont, NY: Eye on Education.

Less Is More

Master teachers focus on quality rather than quantity.

Robyn R. Jackson, 2009, p. 4

Scenario
Wizards, Elves, and Knights

Ms. Sanchez was scrambling around trying to finish grading the last of the homework. Seven months into her first year teaching, she had found that things just never seemed to slow down.

Ms. Robinson, her mentor, came into the room. "Hey girl, you're going to be late to the faculty meeting again."

"I know," Ms. Sanchez replied. "I just can't seem to catch up, and maybe if I avoid the meeting, they won't add any new work for me. Every faculty meeting, there seems to be one new thing to add to my weekly schedule. First mandatory weekly safety training, then that consultant with more test taking tips and techniques and last month we got cursive writing added to our weekly schedule, just because some school board member thought it would be a good idea to practice cursive writing for 30 minutes a week. I don't even remember how to do cursive writing and what am I going to leave out if I spend an extra 30 minutes on that?"

"I know it can be frustrating, even after 22 years teaching, I still am not fond of faculty meetings," Ms. Robinson responded. "And I certainly don't care for it when they try to add things to the schedule."

"So how do you manage that?" Ms. Sanchez asked.

"Well for one thing, I try to fit the new things into the schedule I already have. Let's head over to the faculty meeting and I will try to explain it."

"Really, you found a way to fit cursive into your regular schedule? Let me hear how that worked." Ms. Sanchez had let a little sarcasm into her voice.

"Well, I'll tell you. Do you know that new book series, the one with the dragons and magicians and elves and things?"

"Sure the kids have been passing the books around class since I picked them up at the used book store."

"Well I heard them playing some game at recess, so I knew they were interested in it."

"You have time for recess?"

"Of course, wouldn't miss it. I learn so much about what the kids are interested in. I see it as a good time investment. So anyway, I went out and got some cheap calligraphy pens. Then I made up some fake parchment paper. Then last week I did a little mini lesson on calligraphy, told them about how books had to be copied by hand; I showed them a couple of examples. Then I brought up the stories from the book series. I told them that they had to imagine they were characters in the books, they could be wizards or elves or knights or whatever. Then they had to either write me their own spells, or tell a story about a brave person, or describe a fanciful creature they had discovered. They worked on drafts on regular paper and then when they were ready they got to check out a pen and parchment to write them down."

"Wow, what a great idea," Ms. Sanchez responded.

"They loved it, worked on it all morning, some even wrote more than one, even Robert who does not care for writing at all. At the end they wanted to put them together into a book, actually three books. Our classroom library now has a book of spells, a book of brave stories, and a book of fanciful creatures. They are the most popular books in class. They asked me if we can do it again this week. So I've covered writing, social studies, and cursive all in one lesson."

"I think I may steal your ideas," Ms. Sanchez said smiling.

"Go right ahead, I can lend you the pens if you want. The thing you have to remember is that sometimes less is more, you can't cram everything into the day, but you can make the teaching you do more efficient."

Ms. Sanchez opened the door into the cafeteria. "I guess that will give me something to think about during the fabulous faculty meeting."

"Oh yeah, one more thing," Ms. Robinson added. "I've got a good article on good homework and bad homework I want to share with you; remind me after the meeting."

Ms. Sanchez smiled again. "Thanks, I really need that," she said as they found a seat at the table with the rest of the fourth-grade teachers.

Too Much to Teach

When the United States has challenges, it looks to its public schools for answers. From the space race with the Soviet Union in the 1950s and 1960s to the current need for technologically prepared workers, schools have tried to meet the nation's needs. Schools are integral in trying to solve an array of social challenges too, including everything from racial integration to obesity. As schools tackle these challenges, they often add more to the curriculum; more science and math, more digital literacy, more diversity education, more nutrition education, drug use prevention, gun safety or control, and so forth. In addition, many policy makers equate rigor with more content. Therefore, in an effort to make the schools' curricula more rigorous, they add more content.

Taxpayers, politicians, and business leaders are also demanding more accountability from the public schools. The No Child Left Behind Law (2001) requires that schools create an accountability system that emphasizes standardized tests. Test preparation and benchmark exams to get ready for the end-of-the-year, high-stakes tests also take tremendous amounts of potential instruction time.

All this produces an overcrowded curriculum. Some call it a curriculum that is a mile wide and an inch deep. "'So much to teach-so little time!' is the cry from many classrooms" (Russell-Bowie, 2009, p. 2).

Some educators view the Common Core State Standards (2010), currently adopted by 43 states, as just one more thing added to the curriculum, making the curriculum more crowded than ever. In reality, the Common Core standards can be used as a springboard for creating a streamlined curriculum that does less, but does it better. Students of all ages learn best when they are actively engaged in their learning (Lujan & DiCarlo, 2006), and when they can be re-energized through breaks, such as recess (Jarrett et al., 1998). However, teachers often feel they need to rush to cover the curriculum and prepare students for high-stakes testing that may impact the students' and teachers' futures. As a result, more time is spent on drill and repetition rather than student-centered learning, and little time is available for non-test related activities, such as music, art, drama, or recess (Russell-Bowie, 2009).

Rigor

Covering more material does not mean that students learn more. In fact, Blackburn (2013), an expert in rigorous education, believes that rigor comes from depth not breadth. Both the overcrowded curriculum and the emphasis on standardized testing result in an erosion of teaching and learning.

- ◆ The breadth of the curriculum is emphasized over the depth of learning.
- ◆ Teachers move on to new concepts before students have an opportunity to master concepts.
- ◆ Teachers do not have time to make necessary adjustments for English language learners, learning disabled, gifted students, or other students with special needs.
- ◆ Students are passive recipients of information rather than active participants in their learning.

♦ Research and project-based learning is diminished or eliminated.

♦ Content not assessed by high-stakes tests is minimized or not covered at all.

♦ Assessment is often reduced to multiple choice and short answer tests that are faster to take and grade.

New Goals

Despite all the changes in society, schools have remained basically the same, placing an emphasis on information rather than processes of learning, problem solving, and collaboration. To engage students more in their own education and provide them with more rigor takes time and a different approach. In this technological age, we can get almost any information we want by speaking into our cell phones or conducting a search on our computer. Students no longer need to memorize facts, instead they need to know what questions to ask, where to find the answers, and how to analyze, synthesize, and share the information found. The Partnership for 21st Century Skills states on their website:

> Every child in America needs to be ready for today's and tomorrow's world. A profound gap exists between the knowledge and skills most students learn in school and the knowledge and skills they need for success in their communities and workplaces. To successfully face rigorous higher education coursework, career challenges and a globally competitive workforce, U.S. schools must align classroom environments with real world environments by fusing the three Rs [reading, writing, and arithmetic] and four Cs [critical thinking and problem solving, communication, collaboration, and creativity and innovation].
>
> (para. 11)

Wagner (2008) came to similar conclusions when he examined *The Global Achievement Gap*. He called for schools to focus on seven survival skills: critical thinking and problem solving, collaboration, agility and adaptability, initiative and entrepreneurialism, effective oral and written communication, accessing and analyzing information, and curiosity and imagination. When we look at our standardized test culture, few of these skills appear anywhere in the curriculum.

Instead of covering more material, elementary school educators need to spend more time on each topic and provide students with the time necessary to explore ideas in-depth and share what they learn. In this case, *less is really more.*

Reasons for Concern

Grade Retention
There are many indications that what we are doing now in U.S. schools is not working. One of them is the rate at which students are being held back a grade. The National Association of School Psychologists estimates that at least 2 million students are held back every year, mostly because they are behind academically (Jimerson, Woehr, Kaufman, & Anderson, 2004). These students are not getting the help they need before they fail.

National Assessment of Educational Progress (the Nation's Report Card)
Despite the reforms that were initiated in 2001 with No Child Left Behind, scores on the National Assessment of Educational Progress (National Center for Education Statistics) in math and reading have risen only slightly. This assessment is often called the Nation's Report Card because it is given to a sampling of students across the country and is seen as a better measurement of students' abilities than the state standardized tests prior to Common Core. In 2011, only 34 percent of fourth-grade students taking the test were rated as proficient in reading and 40 percent were proficient in math. The writing test was not given to fourth graders, but only 24 percent of eighth graders made the proficient level. Just as disturbing is the continued gap between white and minority students. The gap on both reading

and math in fourth grade was about 24 points on a 500-point scale.

International Comparisons

In addition, the United States has consistently ranked below many other countries in the areas of reading, mathematics, and science on the Program for International Student Assessment (PISA, 2012). PISA assesses 15-year-old students from 65 countries and educational systems. Nineteen of the groups assessed ranked above the United States in reading, 29 educational systems had higher average scores in math, and 22 surpassed the United States in science literacy in 2012. While the great majority of countries have seen improvements in their scores over the last decade, the U.S. scores have remained flat (Gurria, 2013). "All over the world, teachers are learning to repackage their curriculum so that students uncover and discover, rather than merely cover material" (Jaeger, 2014, p. 18).

High School Graduation Rates

High school graduation rates are at their highest level in 20 years, but many students are still being left behind in an era when a high school diploma is the minimum needed to secure a job. Nationally, about 72 percent of students graduate from high school but among African Americans, Latinos, and American Indians, the average is 56 percent. About 1.2 million students per year don't earn a diploma ("Rising graduation rate," 2011).

The Education Trust argues that in order to close the achievement gap, the education for all students must be improved. "If we are going to close America's long-standing gaps in achievement, we need not only to bring up our low performing low-income students and students of color, but also to accelerate our middle and high performers to even higher levels of achievement," (Bromberg & Theokas, 2013, p. 2).

Lack of Preparation for College

Even students who graduate are often not prepared for life after high school. The ACT college readiness assessment results indicate that only a third of students taking the exam at the end of high school have the skills needed for college but two-thirds of them are entering college. Many lack the basic knowledge and skills necessary to succeed in college courses. As a result, increasing numbers of students are required to take remedial courses in math, reading, and/or writing before they can begin their actual college studies. In 2012, about 40 percent of incoming freshman needed to take at least one remedial course in college ("College preparedness lacking," 2012).

During the industrial age, people could find good-paying jobs without a post-secondary education, but that is no longer true. Wagner estimates that "85 percent of current jobs and almost 90 percent of the fastest growing and best paying jobs now require postsecondary education" (2008, p. xx). In the past, people often worked with their hands but now the workplace requires people with critical thinking skills. Since machines and computers have taken over many of the manual tasks at factories, people are now needed to program and repair the machines, solve problems, and collaborate with other employees.

Lack of Preparation for Jobs

Although the unemployment rate is currently high in the United States, some employers are having trouble filling positions because students are not prepared for the job market ("Three million open jobs," 2012). The workforce is lacking in three major areas: basic academic skills, intrapersonal and interpersonal skills, and specific job-related skills. Specific job-related skills are beyond the scope of this book, but the foundation for the basic academic, intrapersonal, and interpersonal skills is built in elementary school. Employers lament that potential employees cannot write, present information to others, or solve problems. Almost all jobs require some reading, writing, or math. Employers would like to have employees who value getting to work on time and doing their best regardless of the position. In addition, some employees lack an ability to analyze their own strengths and weaknesses and their needs for learning and growth. Most jobs also value people who can work well in a team and/or with clients and customers.

Importance of Elementary School

Elementary school may seem a little early to think about preparing students for college or the job market, but the foundation is set in elementary school. Attitudes and work habits become more and more difficult to change as students grow older. For example, students who are not accustomed to working in a team in elementary school may find collaboration challenging when they get to high school and beyond. Students who believe they only need to do enough to pass the test will not suddenly develop the curiosity necessary to learn more about a topic and share that information with others when they reach college or the workforce. Wagner (2008) writes, "It's really tough to teach children how to think differently if they've spent ten years on one level of thinking and then they go to college" (p. 17). Many education reform efforts have focused on high school, but for some students that may be too late.

The Common Core standards are designed to provide "clear signposts along the way to the goal of college and career readiness for all students"(Common Core State Standards, 2010). The overarching goals in the language arts, even for elementary school, are called "Common Core College and Career Readiness Anchors." There are specific objectives within the anchors that become increasingly more complex and difficult through the grade levels, but the goal is to help students become ready for college and careers beginning in kindergarten.

The Important Stuff

Although many educators agree that the curriculum is overcrowded, they don't know what to cut. Instead of thinking about what to cut first, educators need to examine their goals for students first. What do we want students to know and, more important, be able to do when they complete school? As Drake (2012) writes, ". . . the only things I truly remember are the things that I have needed to use in later life" (p. 1). Most educators and employers agree that the emphasis should be on learning to read deeply, speak and write clearly, and problem solve rather than on memorizing specific facts. Students need to learn to ask questions, find answers, and evaluate those answers. The processes of learning should be the goal in elementary school, and the content a means to that goal. For example, it is not important to read every selection in a textbook, but it is important that students learn to read a variety of texts with deep comprehension. The quantity of research that students do using the Internet is not as important as students learning how to judge the validity of the information they find.

The Common Core supports this view of the learning process. Harris (2013) did a study of the words used in the Common Core standards and found that they emphasized what students could "do" far more than what they "know." The standards emphasize more in-depth learning. For example, by second grade, students are expected to "compare and contrast two or more versions of the same story." By fifth grade, students are expected to "conduct short research projects that use several sources to build knowledge through investigation of different aspects of a topic." These are just two examples of Common Core standards that demand educators to spend more time on fewer topics.

In elementary school, where students usually only have one or two teachers, it is also effective to integrate content as the teacher in the scenario at the beginning of the chapter did. For example, students can learn to read and make charts and graphs as a part of a social studies or science unit rather than as a separate lesson. The Common Core also supports this integration of content in the elementary school. There are no separate elementary school standards for science or social studies. Instead, the standards promote "literacy in history/social studies, science, and technical subjects."

Less Is More takes a practical look at reducing the overcrowding in the elementary school curriculum and the time used specifically for test preparation. It provides suggestions that will allow teachers to meet current curriculum requirements and help prepare their students for standardized testing without sacrificing student engagement and motivation. *Less Is More* is about preparing students for a world in which they need to read with understanding, solve complex problems, communicate orally and in writing, and collaborate with others face-to-face and virtually.

Preview of the Chapters

Chapter 2: Cutting, Combining, and Slowing Down

Chapter 2 explains ways to set goals for student learning and cut practices that do not support those goals. Integrating the curriculum, the focus of the chapter, is the key to doing less but doing it more effectively. The chapter discusses how schools implementing the Common Core can use it as a springboard for curriculum integration. By covering fewer topics, educators and students alike have the time to slow down and explore topics in depth.

Chapter 3: Critical Readers and Researchers

The type of reading and research skills needed today are very different from 20 years ago. Today, there is an abundance of information available, but students need to be able to evaluate the source and content of what they read. In general, elementary schools already are doing a good job of teaching students to decode words and determine literal meaning. Chapter 3 discusses ways to help students take the next step and become critical readers and researchers.

Chapter 4: Problem Solvers and Decision Makers

Problem solving, decision making, and planning skills are needed throughout life. Chapter 4 discusses ways that students can use a problem-solving process in math as well as other content areas. Spaced repetition and interleaving based on recent brain research help students develop and remember problem solving, decision making, and planning skills.

Chapter 5: Effective Communicators

If we ask employers what they consider to be the greatest weakness of potential employees, they will almost always respond that today's graduates lack effective communication abilities, especially writing skills. Chapter 5 explains how teachers can find the time for students to do authentic writing and still prepare for high-stakes testing. In addition, the chapter suggests ways to improve students' oral communication and presentation skills.

Chapter 6: Engaged Learners

When students are engaged in their learning, they spend more time on assigned tasks and have higher achievement. Chapter 6 explains how *less is more* motivates students to become engaged learners. The chapter also explores ways students can become reflective and self-regulating, abilities that are needed if they are to become independent, lifelong learners.

Chapter 7: Collaborators

Students are more motivated, learn more, think more deeply, and remember longer when they work with other students. As students collaborate, the teacher is free to work with individuals or small groups. Chapter 7 provides a framework for the purposeful integration of teamwork skills into student work projects and assignments, providing them with a strong foundation for their future.

Chapter 8: Getting the Most Out of Assessment

This chapter provides practical suggestions for effective assessment in the elementary school classroom during this era of high-stakes assessments. Chapter 8 explores assessment during instruction to provide information for instruction and student feedback. It also discusses ways of preparing students for end of the year standardized tests without sacrificing critical thinking, problem solving, research, and in-depth reading and writing.

Chapter 9: Differentiation

Perhaps one of the greatest challenges for teachers today is meeting the diverse needs of all students, who have various levels of academic, social, emotional, physical, and English abilities. Spending more time on fewer topics allows teachers to better meet the needs of students. Chapter 9 explains how to maintain high expectations for all students but to modify instruction and assessment to ensure all students learn and progress.

Chapter 10: Supporting Teachers Doing Less

If *less is more* ideas are to succeed, they must have the support of the educational leaders in the school and district. Chapter 10 suggests ways that educational leaders can build the capacity and culture needed for the success of these ideas. This chapter specifically looks at ways to find time for teacher collaboration and how to develop Professional Learning Communities.

Chapter 11: Families, Communities, and Schools Working Together

Family and community support is essential for the success of change in schools. Chapter 11 focuses on ways of building trust with families and community members through two-way communication. The chapter explains important issues of family and community engagement during a time of change and high-stakes assessment.

Chapter 12: Overcoming Obstacles

Implementing new learning standards such as the Common Core and striving to raise student achievement test scores is very demanding and has created additional pressures on teachers and schools. Chapter 12 explores some of the challenges, such as the emphasis on high-stakes testing, the need for more technology, and finding teacher collaboration time. Ideas for overcoming these challenges are presented.

Chapters 2 through 12 all include practical examples of the ways the ideas in this book can be applied. They also provide resources for learning more about the topics discussed.

Chapter 13: Ten Keys to *Less Is More*

Chapter 13 helps to put all the ideas presented in this book together and provides a summary of how educators and policy makers can actually improve education by doing less. This book does not assume policy changes; instead it provides feasible ideas to achieve more by doing less in the current educational climate.

References

Blackburn, B. (2013, February 12). *How to tackle the challenges of rigor and the common core* [Webinar]. Retrieved from www.eyeoneducation.com

Bromberg, M., & Theokas, C. (2013). *Breaking the glass ceiling of achievement for low income students and students of color.* Retrieved from www.edtrust.org/sites/edtrust.org/files/Glass_Ceiling_0.pdf

College preparedness lacking, forcing students into developmental coursework, prompting some to drop out (2012, June 18). Retrieved from www.huffingtonpost.com/2012/06/18/students-lacking-college-_n_1606201.html

Common Core State Standards (2010). National Governors Association Center for Best Practices, Council of Chief State School Officers. Retrieved from www.corestandards.org/the-standards

Drake, S.M. (2012). *Creating standards-based integrated curriculum: The Common Core State Standards edition* (3rd ed.). Thousand Oaks, CA: Corwin.

Gurria, A. (2013, December 3). A USA and international perspective on 2012 PISA results. Retrieved from www.oecd.org/unitedstates/a-usa-and-international-perspective-on-2012-pisa-results.htm

Harris, B. (2013, March 26). *7 easy-to use-conversational strategies for the Common Core* [Webinar]. Retrieved from www.eyeoneducation.com

Jackson, R.R. (2009). *Never work harder than your students & other principles of great teaching.* Alexandria, VA: ASCD.

Jaeger, P. (2014). The wrong villain. *School Library Journal, 60*(1), 18.

Jarrett, O.S., Maxwell, D.M., Dickerson, C., Hoge, P., Davies, G., & Yetley, A. (1998). Impact of recess on classroom behavior: Group effects and individual differences. *The Journal of Educational Research, 92*, 121–126.

Jimerson, S.R., Woehr, S.M., Kaufman, A.M., & Anderson, G.E. (2004). *Grade retention and promotion: Information and strategies for educators.* National Association of School Psychologists. Retrieved from www.nasponline.org/resources/instruction_curriculum/retentionho_educators.pdf

Lujan, H. L., & DiCarlo, S. E. (2006). Too much teaching, not enough learning: What is the solution? *Advanced Physiology Education, 30*(1), 17–22. Retrieved from www.advan.physiology.org/content/30/1/17.full

National Center for Education Statistics. *National Assessment of Educational Progress (NAEP).* Institute of Education Sciences. Retrieved from http://nces.ed.gov/nationsreportcard/about/

No Child Left Behind (2001). Retrieved from www2.ed.gov/nclb/overview/intro/execsumm.html

The Partnership for 21st Century Skills. FAQ. Retrieved from www.p21.org/about-us/p21-faq

The Program for International Student Assessment (PISA, 2012). National Center for Education Statistics, Institute of Education Sciences. Retrieved from http://nces.ed.gov/surveys/pisa/

Rising graduation rate shows continuing progress in school (2011). *American Teacher, 96*(1), 7.

Russell-Bowie, D. (2009). Syntegration or disintegration? Models of integrating the arts across the primary curriculum. *International Journal of Education & the Arts, 10*(28), 1–23. Retrieved from www.ijea.org/v10n28/

Three million open jobs in U.S., but who's qualified? (2012, November 11). CBS News 60 Minutes. Retrieved from www.cbsnews.com/video/watch/?id=50134943

Wagner, T. (2008). *The global achievement gap: Why even our best schools don't teach the new survival skills our children need—and what to do about it.* New York, NY: Basic Books.

Other Resource
Common Core information. www.edutopia.org/common-core-state-standards-resources

2

Cutting, Combining, and Slowing Down

A designer knows he has achieved perfection not when there is nothing left to add, but when there is nothing left to take away.

Antoine de Saint-Exupery

Scenario
More Thinking

Ms. Magnus has been a principal at Washington Elementary School for eight years and oversaw the implementation of the Common Core standards at her school two years ago. Although it appeared on a superficial level that the implementation had gone well, she didn't feel they were really getting to the essence of the standards, higher-order thinking. Teachers felt they needed to cover too much material, and they didn't give students the types of reading, writing, problem solving, and projects that would encourage in-depth research and thinking.

Ms. Magnus knew that something had to be cut in order to focus on the things that she and most of the teachers really felt were important for the students. She began researching ways to help teachers cut and combine lessons in order to achieve their goals and the goals of the Common Core standards. Ms. Magnus decided that it was important for educators at the school to work together to do backwards planning, coming up with goals for the students before they began to cut or combine.

Backwards Planning

Backwards planning begins with goals for students and then works backwards to determine what students should be able to do at each grade level. Our emphasis is on what students can "do" rather than "know" because if they can ask questions, find answers to those questions, and evaluate those answers, they don't need to memorize much information.

> As the knowledge base expands through the use of mass media and technology, the emphasis of education is changing from learning and remembering facts, which will soon be out of date, to understanding the underlying concepts, applying them to new situations, and being able to develop generic skills such as research, analysis, synthesis, evaluation, problem solving, teamwork, leadership, and critical thinking to live and work in tomorrow's world.
>
> (Russell-Bowie, 2009, p. 3)

The authors of this book chose five goals that we believe will help students meet or exceed the Common Core State Standards (2010) and other state standards as well as prepare them for a productive life. We would like students to be: critical readers and researchers, problem solvers, effective communicators, engaged learners, and collaborators. Each of these is explained further in other chapters of this book.

Once the educators have determined the school goals, they should meet in grade-level teams to determine what portions of those goals will be completed at their grade level, using the Common Core or other state standards as a guide. Then teachers will need to meet with teachers in grades below and above their grade level to make sure the curriculum is vertically aligned, that each grade level builds on the last one to reach the school goals by the end of elementary school. (Chapter 10 provides ideas on finding time for teacher collaboration.)

Educators can use the goals as criteria for determining what should be in the curriculum. If a lesson doesn't help achieve the goals, then it should be modified to help meet the goals or be eliminated.

Cutting

Cutting is not easy even with clearly defined goals. What worked in the past may not work as well in the present or future, especially with the increased pressures of high-stakes testing and Common Core. In addition, educational practices that are continued should do more than "work," they should have the greatest impact possible on student learning for the time expended.

Educators need to look at the teaching practices that have the most impact on students' learning and will help students reach the school's goals. A great deal of research is available on which practices improve student achievement and which do not. For example, Hattie's (2012) *Visible Learning for Teachers* examines 150 different practices for their impact on students. In his book, students' expectations for themselves ranks number one. Hattie explains that teachers should find out about students' expectations, encourage them to do even better, and provide them with the assistance needed to reach the goal. This shows students that the teacher values their goals and gives them confidence to reach or exceed them.

In addition to tradition, guilt also holds many teachers back from cutting. In his *80/20 Principle,* Koch says that guilt plays a major role in preventing us from focusing on priorities. Educators often feel if they just work a little harder the students in their class will learn more. Koch says we need to learn to dissociate "effort from reward" (p. 1). For educators this means that teaching more is not the same as students learning more. In reality, students learn more when they, not the teacher, are doing most of the work and when they can spend more time on fewer important things.

Teachers also may feel guilty if they don't cover everything in the textbook. For example, it is customary in elementary school to cover a different selection every week from the reading text. However, there usually is no real reason that teachers need to cover a selection a week. Perhaps they want to read a selection in the reading text one week and then the next week read a selection on a similar topic from the social studies or science textbooks, text sets, or the Internet during the time usually devoted to reading. The number of math problems completed also can be reduced to allow students to understand the problem-solving process. Students can do fewer writing assignments but take time to revise and edit some drafts.

Cutting is hard work but it is essential if educators want to stop rushing to cover more and more material. Something simply has to go.

Combining

Integrating the curriculum is the key to doing less but doing it more effectively. By combining topics and cutting out repetition, educators and students have the time necessary to delve into topics more deeply. Examples of integrated unit outlines are provided at the end of the chapter.

Many people assume that elementary school classes already have integrated curriculum because students usually have one teacher for multiple subject areas. However, this often is not true. There are usually separate standards, textbooks, times, and assessments for each of the different content areas. In fact, at some elementary schools, teachers are expected to be covering a specific topic at a specific time of day if an administrator walks in.

Integrated curriculum is known by different names and takes many forms, but it always provides students with clear connections between different subject areas (Drake, 2012). One of the names for integrated curriculum is synergistic learning, which reflects the idea that the whole in an effectively integrated curriculum is greater than the parts. We are promoting an integrated curriculum that provides extended time on topics so that students have an opportunity to develop critical reading and writing, problem solving, research, and other skills that they will need later in life. In the past, some people opposed integrated curriculum because they felt that everything needed to be taught through thematic units and that all subject areas needed to be included in every thematic unit. We believe that there will be times when concepts need to be introduced discretely. This is especially true with many math concepts that are taught sequentially in elementary school. Not all subject areas need to be included in every unit either; teachers should not make artificial connections or neglect important instruction simply because it does not fit into a unit. The type of integrated curriculum that we are discussing offers many advantages over teaching each subject separately.

- ◆ An integrated curriculum better reflects real life where issues are not separated into reading, writing, math, social studies, science, and so forth.
- ◆ Students learn better because teachers make the connections between subject areas clearer.
- ◆ Achievement is higher when science and social studies are integrated with reading and writing.
- ◆ Teachers are able to include all subject areas, including the arts, in an integrated curriculum rather than just teaching the tested subjects.
- ◆ Skills learned in one subject area are applicable in a variety of subject areas as well as later in life.
- ◆ Curriculum is usually more relevant and motivating because skills are taught in authentic contexts rather than just being learned in isolation on worksheets.
- ◆ An integrated curriculum saves time by removing duplication in different subject areas.
- ◆ Teachers and students have time to go into more depth about fewer topics.

One of the biggest problems of an overcrowded curriculum is a lack of time to teach everything. As Kinniburgh and Byrd (2008) write, ". . . integrating the curriculum makes more sense today than ever before. Teachers must practice teaching smarter rather than harder" (p. 36). When objectives from different subject areas are included in one lesson, it takes less time than teaching each objective in a separate lesson. This time can then be used to go into more depth and allow students to be active rather than passive learners. Spending more time on topics means that students can learn about different perspectives, read multiple texts on the same topic, and complete the writing process rather than just completing drafts before moving onto the next topic.

The Common Core standards, as well as standards from professional organizations such as the National Council for Teachers of Mathematics and the National Council of Teachers of English, correlate well with integrated curriculum. The Common Core does not have separate standards for science and social studies in elementary school. Instead, the science and social studies standards are woven into the literacy and mathematics standards. For example, there are reading standards for informational text, kindergarten through fifth grade.

Slowing Down: The Transition Period

Moving from a traditional curriculum to an integrated curriculum takes time. No matter how great an idea may be, if it is implemented too quickly, it is likely to gather resistance and fail. Teachers often do not have the professional development, planning time, or materials to make changes quickly. Therefore, we begin with transitional steps.

A Little at a Time

Educational leaders and teachers may want to focus on one of their student goals at a time. A principal that I recently talked with said her school was "initiatived" to death by directives from central office. As a result, the educators couldn't implement any of them well. In keeping with *less is more,* educators may want to emphasize one or two of their student goals each year, depending on their priorities. For example, if educators believe their students really need more work on problem solving, they would focus on doing less better in the area of problem solving by cutting out the number of problems presented and emphasizing an understanding of the problem-solving process.

Another good way of making the transition is to try just one integrated unit the first year. This way the teachers can find out what works well and what problems they encounter before trying integrated units all year long. If each teacher in a grade level tries a different unit, the grade-level teachers can get together and combine their efforts.

Integrate Current Topics

Teachers also may look at how they can integrate topics already being taught. For example, are there texts in the reading book that correlate with a science or social studies unit that is usually taught? Can students write about a science experiment that they did? Are there math concepts that can be reinforced during science or social studies?

Divide Work

Teachers may also consider introducing a topic to the whole class and then having different groups of students pursue different aspects of the topic and report back to the class. Thus students share their expertise from their research with the class, but the whole class does not do all the reading, research, or writing on all aspects of the topic. For example, the whole class may be introduced to a unit on the human body. Then the class can be broken into groups and each group can focus on different systems, such as the respiratory system or the digestive system. There are even educational videos online to help young children learn about science and social studies before they know how to read more complex informational text on their own.

Test Preparation

Test preparation is another area in which teachers and educational leaders can make changes during the transitional period. In order to prepare students for high-stakes testing, many teachers use prepared worksheets in the format of the test. In most cases, each of these worksheets has a different topic so students are moving from one topic to another daily with each new worksheet without developing background knowledge, vocabulary, or in-depth understanding of the concepts addressed. If more practice with the test format is needed, it is better to develop test format assignments that correlate with the topics being discussed in class. The test practice then not only helps prepare the students for the exams but also reinforces the vocabulary and concepts being covered in class.

Scheduling

Scheduling is another issue that needs to be addressed before a fully integrated curriculum is implemented. The specific issues and solutions will vary among schools, but the following are some of the challenges that schools may face in scheduling when they implement integrated curriculum. Some schools are moving to departmentalization of subject areas as early as kindergarten. This makes curriculum integration much more difficult than when one teacher instructs the same students most of the day.

Another scheduling issue is pull-out programs for special needs students. For instance, it will no longer be possible to pull a student out of the class during "reading time" because reading will be integrated throughout the day. Students also need to have access to computers for research projects and differentiated instruction, so scheduled visits to a computer lab once or twice a week are probably not enough, especially when that time is used for a predetermined computer program that is not integrated with the units.

Teachers need to have flexibility to organize their time. For example, teachers may want to prepare students for an experiment, do the experiment, clean up from the experiment, and discuss or write about what they learned, which requires extended amounts of time. This is easier in elementary school than middle school or high school but still requires some thinking so that all teachers have blocks of uninterrupted teaching time.

Planning Integrated Units

Choosing Topics

Once teachers are ready to plan the units, they can begin by working with other grade-level teachers to decide what themes or problems they want to explore (Roberts & Kellough, 2008).

This requires a different way of thinking than is usually involved in planning. Teachers should remember that it is not important how many activities they do, how much information is covered, or how many assignments students complete, it is much more important that students are given opportunities for deep reading, problem solving, writing, research, and collaboration. The themes and lessons should engage students and help them reflect on their own learning.

Teachers may look at standards, objectives, or textbooks for various subject areas and see how they can be combined. For example, a theme on point of view could easily be applied to literature, social studies, and art. Teachers may also want to look at local problems that interest the students. For instance, there is a local reservoir near us that has fish contaminated by chemicals. This would make an interesting problem for upper elementary grade students to explore. After grade-level teachers have drafted a list of theme topics, teachers need to meet across grade levels to avoid too much duplication or leaving huge gaps in the students' knowledge. When teachers know that students will study a theme in the grade level before or after them, they may feel more comfortable in cutting that from their grade-level curriculum in order to spend more time on fewer topics. This vertical alignment helps to ensure coordination and continuity not only within grade levels but between them.

Each theme will require extended periods of instructional time with no less than three weeks being devoted to a theme. Instructional time is needed so concepts and vocabulary can be developed, students can be actively engaged, and questions can be investigated. Therefore, most schools would not have more than 12 themes in a year and fewer themes would allow more in-depth study. Themes also may be related. For example, teachers may do a longer unit on health and safety, and then divide the unit into smaller themes covering nutrition, exercise, hygiene, and safety.

Topic Questions

After themes have been selected, teachers should develop questions that will be explored during the unit (Drake, 2012). These questions should be open-ended with a variety of correct responses. If the teachers cannot think of questions that will encourage deep thinking then the unit is probably not appropriate. For example, Valentine's Day probably is not a good theme, but close to Valentine's Day, the teachers could do a theme on friendship. Questions would include: What makes a good friend? What do I do with my friends? What causes problems between friends? Teasing and lying may also be discussed as part of this unit. Related stories and nonfiction selections can be read aloud by the teacher and silently by the students.

If there are some topics that are supposed to be covered every year by teachers, such as bully prevention, try to integrate them into one of the other themes each year. In the early grades, bully prevention might be included in a unit on feeling good about myself, and in the upper elementary grades, during a unit on peace.

Reading and Writing across the Curriculum

When themes have been chosen and questions posed, the teachers can look at their reading and writing curriculum. All of the reading and writing objectives or standards should be taught and/or reinforced sometime during the year through the units. Most should be integrated into several units. Some units lend themselves better to some objectives than others. For example, the Common Core and many state standards require students to find the reasons that an author uses to support specific points. This is best done when the author takes a specific point of view or is making an argument. Some standards, such as reading foundational skills, may need to be taught in isolation first but should then be reinforced as students are reading texts as part of integrated units.

Mathematics

With math concepts, elementary school teachers often need to introduce the concepts first and then apply them during the units. Instead of using all the practice problems in the math book, students can practice their math skills as part of the themes. Problem solving, measurement, fractions and percentages, and representing and interpreting data are all easily integrated into many units.

At one time, there was a great deal of pressure to integrate everything into themes. Teachers would make superficial changes to include all subjects in each unit. This did not help students make connections or think deeply. For example, teachers might put raindrops around math problems to make them part of a unit on weather. There are many better ways of integrating math into a unit on weather, depending on the grade level of the students. Younger students might go outside to take the temperature, check a rain gauge, or measure the amount of snow on the ground. For more advanced students, it might mean finding the average high temperature for the last week.

Lesson Planning

Once the units have been outlined, teachers can begin determining what will be included in specific lessons. Rather than thinking of lessons in 45- to 60-minute units as is often done, educators can look at what learning they want to occur during the unit and how this is best accomplished. Although lessons will need to be divided into daily sessions, one lesson could go on for several days. This is how the integrated unit delves into topics in more depth. Although activities should be engaging, teachers need to be careful about doing activities that are motivating but do not significantly advance learning. Too many times students complete activities, such as science experiments, without understanding the purpose of the experiment. Therefore, it is important to prepare students before activities and conduct follow-up after the activities. One of the authors conducts school group tours at a local nature center. Although the tours themselves are educational, it is obvious when students have been prepared before the tour and when they know that they will be asked to discuss or write about the experience afterwards. Other groups look at the tours as a day off from school and get much less out of the experience.

The resources available today for thematic units are almost overwhelming. In addition to traditional resources, there are a myriad of online ones, including information, videos, interactive activities, photos, and more that teachers can use or students can search when doing online research, such as Webquests. One of the problems with online material is that much of it is written above the level of elementary school students. However, some websites provide information about the target age groups of the online information, such as Webquests and educational video sites. (A few such websites are provided under Other Resources at the end of the chapter.)

Assessment is often thought of as something that is separate from instruction, but most assessment can be integrated into instructional activities and provide students and teachers with continuous feedback on their progress. For example, students can role-play historical figures, create dioramas to show the setting of a fictional book, or debate the pros and cons of an issue. Checklists or rubrics can be used to grade these activities. Students should receive the checklist or rubric before beginning the project so they are clear on the teachers' expectations. Although students will need some experience with the format of the standardized tests they will take, most assessments should be open-ended and provide students with opportunities to think critically and creatively. In contrast, multiple-choice questions, by definition, have one correct answer, and their use should be limited.

When considering unit activities and assessments, teachers should again apply backwards planning by looking at their goals and deciding what students will need to know and do to reach those goals. In order to do this, teachers also need to know where students are starting so they don't assume they know more than they do or waste time going over concepts they have mastered. Students sometimes fail at an assignment, not due to lack of effort, but because they lack experience in one or more of the components of the assignment. Let's suppose that small groups of students will be asked to prepare and present a PowerPoint presentation as part of the unit. This seems like a relatively simple assignment for upper grade students but actually involves many components. What do they need to know before they can complete this assignment successfully? They will need to know how to work in a group to complete a project, how to conduct research and evaluate the validity of sources, how to summarize the information gathered, how to prepare a PowerPoint including graphics, and how to present to their peers. Each of these components could be further divided into many specific tasks. The teacher should make expectations clear and demonstrate how he wants the assignment completed, including examples of successfully completed projects. As students are working on the project, he should carefully monitor their progress and provide assistance to individuals or groups who are struggling.

Conclusion

The key to *less is more* is cutting and combining topics. When teachers are covering less, they are able to slow down and allow students to delve into topics more deeply; conducting research, solving problems, and sharing information with others. The following sample units are outlines to provide ideas of how integrated units could be created at different elementary school grade levels. Teachers could create similar outlines for their units before developing daily lessons.

Sample Unit Outlines

Sample Kindergarten Unit
Topic: Basic Animal Needs

Sample Questions
What do animals need to live?
What are differences between wild and domestic animals?
What different habitats do wild animals live in?
How have wild animals adapted to their habitats?
How do people help and hurt animals in the wild?

Sample Activities/Assessments
a) Invite a speaker from a conservation group or a nature center who understands how to present to kindergarteners. Before the speaker comes, have the class come up

with questions for the speaker, which will be written on chart paper. Then send the questions to the speaker so he can be prepared for them. Prepare individual students to ask the questions while the speaker is there. After the guest presentation, write a class book about the topic. The teacher can take dictation from the students and transfer the writing to individual pages that students can illustrate.

b) Provide students with photos or clipart of animals that the class has studied. Then have them glue them onto paper and draw a picture around the animals, representing the appropriate habitat for that animal. Students can show and explain their drawings to the class.

c) Create a center or small group activity in which students sort pictures of animals into wild and domestic animals and then count the number of animals in each group.

Sample Home-School Connections

Send home a note in students' home language encouraging the family to observe animals outside. These could include insects, such as ants or butterflies, birds, or larger animals, such as deer in more rural areas. Students can draw some of the animals seen and bring the pictures in to share with the class.

Sample Common Core Standards

Speaking and Listening Standards K, 3: Ask and answer questions in order to seek help, get information, or clarify something that is not understood.

K, 5: Add drawings or other visual displays to descriptions as desired to provide additional detail.

K, 6: Speak audibly and express thoughts, feelings, and ideas clearly.

Math Standard K, 7: Classify objects into given categories: count the numbers of objects in each category and sort the categories by count.

Sample First-Grade Unit
Topic: Healthy Choices

Sample Questions
What can we do to stay in good health?
What are the nutritional values of different foods?
Why is exercise important?
What are different ways of getting exercise?

Sample Activities/Assessments
a) The teacher reads aloud a children's book about healthy eating, such as *The Berenstain Bears and Too Much Junk Food* (Berenstain & Berenstain, 1985). Discuss the main idea and key details. After the discussion, have students work in pairs to complete a graphic organizer with main ideas and details. If it is more appropriate, they can use drawings and labels in the graphic organizer.

b) Discuss healthy snacks with the students. Choose three of those snacks and survey students to determine which is their favorite. Give each student a sticky note and have them draw their favorite from the three choices. Then place the sticky notes on a bar graph. Have students discuss how many people chose each snack, which is the most popular and which is the least popular, and compare the numbers in the three categories. If possible, enjoy healthy snacks in class. Of course, take into consideration students' food allergies and eating restrictions.

c) Teach the students some simple steps to music. Then have them create their own steps, individually or in pairs, and teach them to the rest of the class. This might be done in conjunction with the physical education teacher.

Sample Home-School Connections
After teaching students about the food pyramid, have students bring in labels from cans, boxes, or other food from home. Students can then place the labels into the correct food categories, according to the government's food pyramid.

Sample Common Core Standards

Speaking and Listening Standard 1, 1: Participate in collaborative conversations with diverse partners about grade-one topics and texts with peers and adults in small and larger groups.

Reading Informational Text Standard 1, 2: Identify the main topic and retell key details of a text.

Math Measurement and Data Standard 1, 4: Organize, represent, and interpret data with up to three categories: ask and answer questions about the total number of data points, how many in each category, and how many more or less are in one category than in another.

Sample Second-Grade Unit

Topic: Reduce, Reuse, and Recycle

Sample Questions

What happens to things we throw away?
How can we reduce what we throw away?
What types of things can we reuse or recycle? How?
How can we reduce our use of water, electricity, gasoline?

Sample Activities/Assessments

a) Bring in items that people usually throw away, such as egg cartons. Have students work in small groups to brainstorm different ways the egg cartons could be reused after the eggs are gone. Then have each group select one of their ideas and create an advertisement, explaining why people should reuse their egg cartons (or other objects) in that way.

b) Conduct research as a class about how electricity use can be reduced. Then look at different uses of electricity within the school. Come up with ideas about how the school can reduce electricity usage. Write a class letter to the principal, suggesting ways to reduce electricity usage at the school.

c) Provide students with grade-appropriate math problems related to the theme. For example, "Matt's water bill was $80 in November. After he cut down his use of water, his bill was $72. How much did Matt save by cutting down the amount of water he uses?" After students have practice with this type of problem, they can work in partners or small groups to come up with their own problems related to the theme.

Sample Home-School Connections

Have students and their families come up with lists of different ways they use water at home. After students bring in their lists, discuss how they could reduce their use of water at home. The class can come up with a list of ways that water use can be reduced. This can be copied, shared with other classes, families, and even sent to the local newspaper.

Sample Common Core Standards

Writing Standards 2, 1: Write opinion pieces in which they introduce the topic or book they are writing about, state an opinion, supply reasons that support the opinion, use linking words (e.g., because, and, also) to connect opinion and reasons, and provide a concluding statement or section.

Writing 2, 7: Participate in shared research and writing projects (e.g., read a number of books on a single topic to produce a report, record science observations).

Math Standard 2, 1: Use addition and subtraction within 100 to solve one- and two-step word problems involving situations of adding to, taking from, putting together, taking apart, and comparing with unknowns in all positions, e.g., by using drawings and equations with a symbol for the unknown number to represent the problem.

Sample Third-Grade Unit

Topic: Fairy Tales

Sample Questions

What are the characteristics of a fairy tale?

How can we identify the main idea or message of a fairy tale?

How do authors develop characters in a fairy tale?

How are fairy tales from different countries similar and different?

Sample Activities/Assessments

a) The teacher reads a fairy tale to the class and helps students to identify the clues to the author's message. The teacher reads another fairy tale and has students participate in Sketch to Stretch (Short, Harste, & Burke, 1996). Students make a sketch, representing the message the author is trying to convey. Students meet in small groups and share their drawing with other students, who explain what they think their peer's drawing means. Then, the artist explains their own interpretation.

b) Read a fairy tale to students and then read a Fractured Fairy Tale based on that story (http://library.loganutah. org/books/children/FracturedTales.cfm). Talk about the differences between the original version of the story and the Fractured Fairy Tale. Provide students with copies of other fairy tales and have them write their own fairy tales by changing characters, settings, endings, or other parts of the original fairy tale.

c) Create or find Readers Theatre scripts based on fairy tales. (Links for websites with Reader's Theater Scripts are provided under other resources.) Divide students into groups based on their reading ability, the difficulty of the script, and the number of parts in the script. Model how to read with expression with students. Provide students with time to read the text repeatedly for fluency rather than memorization. Using the script, students can perform the Reader's Theater for other students in the class and/or a class of younger students.

Sample Common Core Standards

Reading Standard for Literature 3, 2: Recount stories, including fables, folktales, and myths from diverse cultures; determine the central message, lesson, or moral and explain how it is conveyed through key details in the text.

Reading Foundational Skills Standard 3, 4b: Read grade-level prose and poetry orally with accuracy, appropriate rate, and expression on successive readings.

Writing Standard 3, 3: Write narratives to develop real or imagined experiences or events using effective technique, descriptive details, and clear event sequences.

Sample Fourth-Grade Unit
Topic: Force and Motion

Sample Questions
What are examples of Newton's three laws of motion?

How do forces, such as gravity, friction, inertia, and centripetal forces, influence motion?

How can designers use information about forces and motion to design more fuel-efficient cars?

Sample Activities/Assessments
a) Watch *Force and Motion* video from PBS LearningMedia (www.pbslearningmedia.org/resource/idptv11.sci.phys. maf.d4kfom/force-and-motion/)

Afterwards, discuss Newton's Three Laws of Motion and the examples given of each in the video. Then have students work in pairs to come up with other examples of each Law of Motion.

b) Discuss and read about gravity and friction (www. physics4kids.com/files/motion_intro.html). Have students work in pairs to design a parachute for an action figure. Go outside or someplace where the parachutes can be tested. Have students time how long it takes the action figure to land after the teacher drops it from a designated height. Use decimals to indicate fractions of a second. Plot the lengths of time from shortest to longest on a line graph. Have students calculate the difference between the action figure that took the shortest

and longest to land. What about the design of the parachutes and the forces of motion that may have caused
this difference? Do the same activity but measure the
distance the action figure landed from a designated
landing circle. Graph the differences in distances from
the circle and determine what factors may have affected
that distance.

c) Have students work in pairs or small groups to research
ways cars are designed to reduce fuel consumption.
Have students draw a car that they think would consume
less fuel than most vehicles currently on the road. They
should write about why they think their car would use
less fuel based on what they have learned about forces
and motion.

Sample Home-School Connections

At school, have students brainstorm what life would be like
with less gravity. Then have students write a story about a
day at their house with less gravity. They can share it with
their family and at school.

Sample Common Core Standards

Reading Standard for Informational Text 4, 4: Determine the
meaning of general academic and domain-specific words
or phrases in a text relevant to a grade-four topic or subject
area.

Writing Standard 4, 1: Write opinion pieces on topics or texts,
supporting a point of view with reasons and information.

Speaking and Listening Standard 4, 2: Paraphrase portions
of a text read aloud or information presented in diverse
media and formats, including visually, quantitatively, and
orally.

Math Operations and Whole Numbers 4, 1: Use the four
operations to solve word problems involving distances,
intervals of time, liquid volumes, masses of objects, and
money, including problems involving simple fractions or
decimals.

Sample Fifth-Grade Unit
Topic: Conflict and Cooperation

Sample Questions
What causes conflicts between individual people?
What are ways of resolving conflict without fighting?
What causes conflicts between nations or groups of people?
Wars?
How do wars impact people's lives?
How can conflicts between nations or groups of people be resolved without wars?

Sample Activities/ Assessments
a) Provide students with basic conflict resolution training, including listening to other viewpoints, summarizing and repeating what other people say to increase understanding, and working out compromises. Model and role-play these skills with the whole class, using scenarios. Then students can work in pairs or small groups applying the same skills to other scenarios. (The school counselor may be able to assist with this activity.)

b) Provide students with proposals that have two or more viewpoints that are relevant to their lives. Each small group will be presented with a different topic. Students will conduct research and then summarize at least three arguments with relevant data in support of the proposal and three against the proposal. Students can then present their findings to the class and take anonymous written votes and do the necessary math to determine what percentage of students in the class support each viewpoint. Examples of topics could include school uniforms, more or less physical education time each week, a ban on the use of plastic bags by businesses, or required separation of recyclables from other trash.

c) Read about conflicts or wars in history from different viewpoints. (For example, the conflicts between Native Americans and European settlers http://questgarden. com/47/47/8/080717124952/). Explain to students that most major conflicts and wars have multiple causes and effects. Use graphic organizers to show cause and effect relationships. Provide students with additional reading about conflicts and have them identify the causes and effects independently.

Sample Home-School Connections

Write a note home in students' home language, if possible, explaining the conflict resolution instruction they have received. Ask families to work with the student on resolving one conflict the student repeatedly has at home, such as the amount of screen time they are allowed, the amount of money they request, doing chores, or arguing with siblings. Students should practice their listening for understanding skills and then see if a compromise can be reached. For example, families may agree to give the student extra money if they do additional chores at home or they may divide a bedroom down the middle with furniture to reduce conflicts with siblings. This activity should be voluntary and care should be taken because this method of conflict resolution may not fit well with some cultures in which the elders make the decisions and do not compromise with children.

Sample Common Core Standards

Reading Standard for Informational Text 5, 6: Analyze multiple accounts of the same event or topic, noting important similarities and differences in the point of view they represent.

Writing Standard 5, 7: Conduct short research projects that use several sources to build knowledge through investigation of different aspects of a topic.

Math Number and Operations Standard 5, 3: Read, write, and compare decimals to the thousandths.

References

Berenstain, S., & Berenstain, J. (1985). *Berenstain bears and too much junk food.* New York, NY: Random House.

Common Core State Standards (2010). National Governors Association Center for Best Practices, Council of Chief State School Officers. Retrieved from www.corestandards.org/the-standards

Drake, S. M. (2012). *Creating standards-based integrated curriculum: The Common Core State Standards edition* (3rd ed.). Thousand Oaks, CA: Corwin.

Hattie, J. (2012). *Visible learning for teachers: Maximizing impact on learning.* New York, NY: Routledge.

Kinniburgh, L. H., & Byrd, K. (2008). Ten black dots and September 11: Integrating social studies and mathematics through children's literature. *Social Studies, 99*(1), 33–36. doi:10.3200/TSSS.99.1.33–36

Koch, R. *The 80/20 principle: Detonating a time revolution.* Retrieved from www.thisbusinessforyou.com/pdf/The80–20Principleby RichardKoch.pdf

Roberts, P. L., & Kellough, R. D. (2008). *A guide for developing interdisciplinary thematic units* (4th ed.). Upper Saddle River, NJ: Pearson.

Russell-Bowie, D. (2009). Syntegration or disintegration? Models of integrating the arts across the primary curriculum. *International Journal of Education & the Arts, 10*(28). Retrieved from www.ijea.org/v10n28/

Short, K., Harste, J., & Burke, C. (1996). *Creating classrooms for authors and inquirers.* Portsmouth, NH: Heinemann.

Other Resources

Educational videos. Retrieved from http://edutube.org/

Exploratorium. Retrieved from www.exploratorium.edu/explore

Fractured fairy tales. Retrieved from http://library.loganutah.org/books/children/FracturedTales.cfm.

Hattie video on student expectations. Retrieved from http://vimeo.com/41465488

Hinde, E. R., Popp, S. E., Jimenez-Silva, M., & Dorn, R. I. (2011). Linking geography to reading and English language learners' achievement in US elementary and middle school classrooms. *International Research in Geographical and Environmental Education, 20*(1), 47–63.

National Council of Teachers of English and the International Reading Association. *NCTE/IRA standards for the English language arts.* Retrieved from www.ncte.org/standards

National Council for Teachers of Mathematics. *Principles and standards for school mathematics.* Retrieved from www.nctm.org/standards/content.aspx?id=26798

PBS learning. Retrieved from www.pbslearningmedia.org/

Peck, S.M. (2010). Not on the same page but working together: Lessons from an award-winning urban elementary school. *The Reading Teacher, 63*(5), 394–403.

Physics for kids. Retrieved from www.physics4kids.com/

Readers Theater scripts. Retrieved from www.aaronshep.com/rt/RTE.html

Readers Theater scripts. Retrieved from www.thebestclass.org/rtscripts.html

Webquests. Retrieved from http://questgarden.com/47/47/8/080717124952/

Webquests. Retrieved from www.thinkquest.org/en/

Webquests. Retrieved from http://webquest.org/findlinks/

Zhbanova, K.S., Rule, A.C., Montgomery, S.E., & Nielsen, L.E. (2010). Defining the difference: Comparing integrated and traditional single-subject lessons. *Early Childhood Education Journal, 38*(4), 251–258.

3

Critical Readers and Researchers

To the critical reader, any single text provides but one portrayal of the facts, one individual's 'take' on the subject matter.

Kurland, 2000, para. 2

Scenario
Taking the Next Step

At a third-grade teachers' meeting with the literacy coach during October, the teachers were all discussing their students' reading. They agreed that the lower grade teachers were doing a great job of teaching basic reading skills. Most of the students could read and comprehend what was explicitly stated in the text at the beginning of the year, but the teachers were stymied about how to move students beyond a literal level of comprehension. The students often could do more advanced skills, such as making inferences on a worksheet, but then had trouble when they had to apply it to more extended texts. The worksheets, which were designed to prepare the students for the end of the year test, didn't seem to engage the students either.

The literacy coach suggested that they try teaching reading, and writing for that matter, through integrated units. They could do about one integrated unit a month and students could read a variety of informational and fictional texts related to the theme. Students would develop vocabulary through multiple exposures to words in different contexts. Reading different sources on the same topic would help students develop deeper understanding of the topics and move beyond a literal level of comprehension. The teachers decided they would each develop an outline of a different unit by January. The reading coach offered to help them find materials and think of ways to encourage critical reading through the units.

Reading as Thinking

Many teachers across the country have similar problems to those depicted in this scenario. Students can understand the literal meaning of the text but have difficulty with critical reading, which is a combination of critical thinking and strategic reading. The characteristics of critical reading are active, not passive reading, interactive, reflective, and analytical (Langer, 1990; Marschall & Davis, 2012). Critical reading is vital for future education and jobs as well as being part of the Common Core standards. "The standards explicitly move kids to thinking as they read, rather than trying to accumulate a slew of details" (Calkins, Ehrenworth, & Lehman, 2012, p. 100).

More Reading
The first step in improving reading comprehension and achieve-ment is to have students read more. "Students who read a lot score better on every imaginable test—the NAEP, the SAT, the ACT. Any standards based reading instruction needs to build in the expectation that students will do a huge volume of reading . . ." (Calkins et al., 2012, p. 70).

The amount of time devoted to reading instruction has dou-bled over the years since the passage of No Child Left Behind (NCLB, 2001). Unfortunately, much of that increased time is spent on doing reading worksheets or similar activities on the computer, especially test preparation materials, which usually do not encourage critical reading. The time spent actually reading texts has increased only 15 percent (Brenner, Hiebert, & Tompkins,

2009). The *less is more* approach supports doing fewer reading worksheets and focusing more on reading a variety of texts. Even small increases in the opportunity to read can lead to big gains in comprehension and knowledge (Hiebert & Pearson, 2013).

The Common Core also emphasizes reading more, especially nonfiction materials. ". . . the Common Core standards support classrooms in which learning to read and reading to learn occur simultaneously and synergistically" (Hiebert & Pearson, 2013, p. 50).

One of the challenges to reading more informational texts is finding different texts on the same topic that reflect the different reading levels of students in the class. ". . . if your school is like most in the nation, many of the nonfiction texts your students are reading are almost surely too hard or too poorly written to engage students intellectually" (Calkins et al., 2012, p. 89). (Possible ways of obtaining needed texts are discussed in Chapter 12).

Silent Reading

To improve students' comprehension, most student reading should be done silently with a purpose. Oral reading places the emphasis on pronunciation of words, which takes the focus off of comprehension. When one student at a time reads aloud, it also occupies a great deal of class time, and the students who are not reading are often off-task. In life, and on high-stakes tests, most reading is silent.

Some teachers are afraid they won't know if students are really reading if they are reading silently. This is why students need a purpose for reading such as checking predictions, answering questions posed before reading, or looking for evidence to support arguments. Discussions or writing following reading help educators ascertain not only that students have read, but also their level of comprehension.

Silent reading also helps students learn to focus in this era of distractions. We live in a digital age; we also live in a distracted age. We are constantly tethered to cell phones, iPads, and emails, each demanding that we stop what we are doing and devote our attention to something else. Even reading this book you may have a sense of urgency to put it down to check on some other source of information. David Ulin in *The Lost Art of Reading* (2010) writes:

> To read, we need a certain kind of silence, an ability to filter out the noise. That seems increasingly elusive in our overnetworked society, where every buzz and rumor is instantly blogged and tweeted, and it is not contemplation we desire but an odd sort of distraction, distraction masquerading as being in the know.
>
> (p. 34)

Now more than ever an ability for deep reading is going to be tested as children grow up with ever more distractions.

Schema and Vocabulary Through Integrated Units

Students need relevant background knowledge or schema and vocabulary to become critical readers. A reader can't analyze a text, compare it to other texts, or determine the author's perspective without first having vocabulary and schema related to the topic. As McGregor (2007) puts it, "Having schema allows our thinking to go deeper, faster" (p. 30).

Vocabulary is closely tied to reading comprehension. A text is considered at a student's instructional level if he knows at least 95 percent of the words. Simply put, students need to know almost all the words in a text to read with comprehension. "Helping children build vivid and vital vocabularies is a crucial goal in helping all children become the very best readers and writers they can be" (Cunningham & Allington, 2011, p. 96).

Although there are many factors impacting the learning of a specific word, most people have to read, hear, or experience a word a dozen or more times in different contexts before they remember it, which is why integrated units are so important. They provide multiple opportunities to reinforce the same words and concepts through read-alouds, silent reading, real experiences, and the arts over a period of time. This contrasts with most reading worksheets or computer reading exercises, which present different topics with each activity, not providing students with enough exposure or variety of contexts to learn and remember the important vocabulary.

During integrated units, teachers can help students build their vocabulary by providing objects, pictures, and activities that will reinforce important words. For example, if a third-grade class is going to do a unit on simple machines, the term "simple machines" may not mean much to them, but a wheel and axle is something all of them will know about. Bring a toy car or a bicycle wheel in and give them time to brainstorm where else they have seen wheels. After the class has a good list of where wheels are found, ask the students why they think someone invented the wheel and why we still use it today. For each of the simple machines, students should be encouraged to give examples where they have seen or used them and why they think people use them. Then when students read and do experiments with simple machines, they will be able to make connections.

Teachers also can help students get more out of their independent reading by teaching them how to figure out unknown words when they encounter them during reading. Younger students may sound out words and then recognize them because the word is already in their listening vocabulary, but as readers mature, most new words are not in their listening vocabularies. Instead, they must depend more on the context surrounding the unknown word to determine its meaning.

Reading Strategies

Less is more also applies to the teaching of reading strategies. There are a number of different strategies that help students analyze text beyond the who, what, and where that are stated in the text. These strategies include such things as predicting, visualizing, synthesizing, and inferring. Although the Common Core standards do not specifically mention some of these strategies, the strategies are a means of helping students reach the higher comprehension goals of the Common Core. Teachers should cover fewer new reading strategies in a year but spend more time developing each one. The important thing is that students learn when and how to use the strategies independently to improve their understanding of a variety of texts.

McGregor (2007) uses what she calls a "launching sequence" as she introduces each new comprehension strategy. She says, "It's no accident that the lessons where I skimp on the beginning are the same lessons where the kids don't perform well at the end" (p. 4). Slowing down and spending more time on each strategy ultimately results in students who are able to apply the strategies during their own reading. For example, a teacher might introduce inferring by bringing in a backpack full of objects, dumping them on a table where all the students can see them, and start asking students about the person who owns the backpack. As students make guesses, the teacher should ask them what evidence they see in the backpack that leads them to believe that. After students understand the strategy using concrete objects, the class can practice together using read-alouds, and then they can move on to use the strategy during partner and individual reading.

At the lower grades as children are learning to read independently, teachers can help them develop critical thinking by reading books aloud and discussing a variety of texts with them. The Fact or Fiction and Inferential Drawing activities at the end of the chapter are examples of how higher-order thinking skills can be encouraged when the teacher reads books aloud.

Perhaps one of the most important strategies for reading is questioning that goes beyond the literal level. Currently, Hattie (2012) reports that 60 percent of questions asked in class involve factual recall and another 20 percent are procedural questions, so only about 20 percent of the questions asked in an average classroom encourage deeper thinking. Not only should teachers ask questions beyond the literal level, students should be able to ask their own higher-order thinking questions.

Critical Researchers

Knowing how to ask questions is especially important as students begin to do research. Before starting a research project, students should know what question or questions they will try to answer.

This provides them with a purpose for reading and helps focus their research. A few decades ago, students often had a hard time finding enough information for their research reports. In contrast, today, students have a plethora of information available on most topics. They need to be able to choose which sources of information will help them answer their questions.

They also need to learn to evaluate the source of information and understand that different texts are written from different perspectives or points of view. Clarke and Whitney (2009) believe that multiple perspectives texts can act as a "bridge to critical literacy" (p. 530). For example, a teacher might introduce *Westward Expansion: An Interactive History Adventure* (Lassieur, 2008), which has three different stories in one book. Students can choose to be a pioneer on the Oregon Trail, a Civil War vet looking for work, or a Sioux warrior. After students have followed each of these characters, they can discuss how their adventures were the same and different. The Multiple Perspectives activity at the end of the chapter provides more ideas for lessons and books.

As older students do research projects, they may be required to present more than one viewpoint on some of their research projects, such as the use of daily multi-vitamins. Some say they are a good supplement for those who don't eat a well-balanced diet while others say they are a waste of money and could even sometimes be harmful. After presenting multiple opinions on a topic, upper elementary grade students can be asked to come to their own conclusions and explain their reasons.

According to Calkins et al. (2012) many of the problems with informational writing are actually not writing problems at all; they are from a superficial reading and understanding of the topic. When students read critically and understand the topic, they will be able to choose the important points and organize the information in a logical manner.

Reading Instruction for Standardized Tests

When students read real texts and are asked to think about the texts critically, they will build the vocabulary and thinking skills that are needed on standardized tests (Owocki, 2012). Although the focus of reading instruction should not be on test preparation, students should have an opportunity to intermittently practice reading and answering questions in the same format that is on the standardized test(s). This provides them with the confidence to be successful on high-stakes testing. It is particularly true with the new computer-administered assessments. Students need practice with the computer so that they are able to show what they understand without being hindered by a lack of familiarity with the format of the test or the use of the computer.

Conclusion

Fewer reading worksheets and more real reading should fill the day in elementary school classrooms. There should be less oral reading and more silent reading for comprehension. Students should read more about fewer topics so that they develop the vocabulary and background knowledge necessary to go beyond a superficial understanding of text. There should be less emphasis on the details presented in the text and more on ideas. Students should be given adequate time and resources to conduct in-depth research. When students become critical readers, they will be able to tackle standardized tests as well as the reading necessary in their future educational and career endeavors. The following are examples that will encourage critical reading.

Sample Lessons

Inferential Drawing

Purpose: To help young children make inferences.

Participants: Kindergarten through first-grade students

Preparation: The teacher should choose a book or section of a book that contains descriptive language about a setting. The setting should be a place that most of your students have been. For example, don't choose a mountain setting if many of the students in the class have not been to the mountains.

Activity Description

1. Tell students that after you finish reading, they will need to draw a picture of where the story took place, which is called the setting.
2. Explain that the author will give them some information about what the place looks like, but not all the details. They will have to use what the author says plus their own minds to decide what to draw.
3. Read a short book or a section of a book that describes one setting without showing students a picture of the setting.
4. Have students draw a picture of where the story takes place.
5. Then have students share their picture with a partner. They should discuss what is the same about the pictures and what is different.
6. Lead students in a discussion that helps them understand that the things that are the same or similar are from what the author said. (For example, if the story took place at a lake, then all the pictures will include a lake.) The things that are different are from their own minds.
7. Explain to students that every time we hear a story or read a story, we fill in details with our own mind. When we do this, it is called making an inference.

Modification: Have students draw a picture of a character based on a description without seeing a picture of the character in the book.

Common Core Reading Anchor 1: Read closely to determine what the text says explicitly and to make logical inferences from it; cite specific textual evidence when writing or speaking to support conclusions from the text.

Common Core Listening Anchor 2: Integrate and evaluate information presented in diverse media and formats, including visually, quantitatively, and orally.

Fact or Fiction?

Purpose: To help young children discriminate between elements of stories that could happen in life and those that the author makes up to make them more interesting.

Participants: Kindergarten through third-grade students

Preparation: Choose a picture book that contains real elements, such as actual animals, and fictional elements, such as the animals talking.

Activity Description

1. Talk to students about how we sometimes pretend when we play. Encourage them to give examples, such as pretending to be a fireman or having a stuffed animal talk. Then explain to them that authors sometimes do the same thing when they write to make the stories more interesting.
2. Tell the students to listen as you read for things that could really happen and other things that are made-up or pretend.
3. Stop a few times during the reading to ask students if things are really possible or made-up.
4. After finishing reading, make a T-chart from the story that shows things from the story that could really happen on one side and made-up things on the other side.

Common Core Reading Anchor 3: Analyze how and why individuals, events, or ideas develop and interact over the course of a text.

Multiple Perspectives

Purpose: To help students understand that the same story can be told from different points of view or perspectives.

Participants: First through fifth-grade students (See notes below for upper grade students.)

Preparation: Find books such as the *Three Little Pigs* that have more than one version available. *The Three Little Pigs* (Galdone, 1984), told by a narrator from the pigs' perspective, *The True Story of the Three Little Pigs* (Scieszka, 1989) told from the wolf's perspective, and *The Fourth Little Pig* (Celsi, 1990) told from the sister's perspective.

Activity Description

1. Read the traditional version of the book aloud and do a story map that shows the problem and solution. This should be on chart paper or another media that can be displayed over several days.
2. Repeat the process on a different day with another version of the story.
3. Lead the students in a discussion of the similarities and differences between the stories, using a Venn Diagram.
4. Ask students why the stories were different even though it was basically the same story.

Extensions: Some books include two different points of view within the same book. For example *The Pain and the Great One* (Blume & Trivas, 1985) is told half by an eight-year-old girl and half by her six-year-old brother who both think the parents like the other one best. Another example is *George vs. George: The American Revolution as Seen from Both Sides* (Schanzer, 2004).

Other books with multiple perspectives at different grade levels can be found in *The Common Core Lesson Book K–5* (Owocki, 2012) or at www.readwritethink.org.

Another method of exploring different perspectives is to use Empathy Maps, originally used in business to see a product or service through another person's perspective. Empathy Maps encourage students to look at how another person thinks, feels, sees, and hears things as well as what that person might say or do under specific circumstances. Empathy Maps also help students explore fictional or real people's goals and challenges to those goals (Bratsberg, 2012).

Common Core Reading Anchor 6: Assess how point of view or purpose shapes the content and style of a text.

References

Blume, J., & Trivas, I. (1985). *The pain and the great one*. New York, NY: Dell.

Bratsberg, H. M. (2012). Empathy Maps of the FourSight Preferences. Creative Studies Graduate Student Master's Projects. Paper 176. Retrieved from http://digitalcommons.buffalostate.edu/cgi/viewcontent.cgi?article=1180&context=creativeprojects

Brenner, D., Hiebert, E. H., & Tompkins, R. (2009). How much and what are third graders reading? In E. H. Hiebert (Ed.), *Reading more, reading better* (pp. 118–140). New York, NY: Guilford Press.

Calkins, L., Ehrenworth, M., & Lehman, C. (2012). *Pathways to the Common Core: Accelerating achievement*. Portsmouth, NH: Heinemann.

Celsi, T. (1990). *The fourth little pig*. Austin, TX: Steck-Vaughn.

Clarke, L. W., & Whitney, E. (2009). Walking in their shoes: Using multiple-perspectives texts as a bridge to critical literacy. *The Reading Teacher, 62*(6), 530–534.

Cunningham, P. M., & Allington, R. L. (2011). *Classrooms that work: They can all read and write* (5th ed.). Boston, MA: Pearson.

Galdone, P. (1984). *The three little pigs*. Boston, MA: HMH Books for Young Readers.

Hattie, J. (2012). *Visible learning for teachers: Maximizing impact on learning*. New York, NY: Routledge.

Hiebert, E., & Pearson, D. (2013). What happens to the basics? *Educational Leadership, 70*(4), 48–36.

Kurland, D. J. (2000). *What is critical reading?* Retrieved from www.criticalreading.com/critical_reading.htm

Langer, J. A. (1990). The process of understanding reading for literary and informative purposes. *Research in the Teaching of English, 24,* 229–260.

Lassieur, A. (2008). *Westward expansion: An interactive history adventure*. North Mankato, MN: Capstone Press.

Marschall, S., & Davis, C. (2012). A conceptual framework for teaching critical reading to adult college students. *Adult Learning, 23*(2), 63–68. doi:10.1177/1045159512444265

McGregor, T. (2007). *Comprehension connections: Bridges to strategic reading*. Portsmouth, NH: Heinemann.

No Child Left Behind (NCLB, 2001). Retrieved from www2.ed.gov/
    nclb/overview/intro/execsumm.html
Owocki, G. (2012). *The Common Core lesson book K-5.* Portsmouth, NH:
    Heinemann.
Schanzer, R. (2004). *George vs. George: The revolutionary war as seen by
    both sides.* Des Moines, IA: National Geographic Children's Books.
Scieszka, J. (1989). *The true story of the 3 little pigs!* New York, NY:
    Scholastic.
Ulin, D. (2010). *The lost art of reading: Why books matter in a distracted
    time.* Seattle, WA: Sasquatch Books.

Other Resources

Hill, R. (2012). All Aboard! Implementing Common Core offers school
    librarians an opportunity to take the lead. *School Library Journal,
    58*(4), 26–30. Retrieved from www.slj.com/2012/03/standards/
    common-core/all-aboard-implementing-common-core-offers-
    school-librarians-an-opportunity-to-take-the-lead/#_
International Reading Association. www.reading.org/
Multiple perspectives texts and lesson plans. Retrieved from www.
    readwritethink.org
National Council of Teachers of English. www.ncte.org/
National Geographic for kids. http://kids.nationalgeographic.com/
    kids/
The Reading and Writing Project. www.readingandwritingproject.com

4

Problem Solvers and Decision Makers

Problem solving is "what you do when you don't know what to do."

Maryellen Weimer, 2010, para. 1

Scenario
The Problem of the Suitcase

A friend of mine came to my apartment one time. She was traveling on an international flight and had to weigh her suitcase to make sure she would not be charged extra if it was too heavy. She knew I had a simple bathroom scale at the time. She put the suitcase on the scale to see how much it weighed, but the suitcase was too large and blocked the dial on the scale. I asked her one quick question and her problem was solved. What did I ask?

Now for people not used to solving problems, this is a difficult problem. However solving this type of problem is extremely important. Developing a new piece of technology or creating something novel involves solving problems that do not have obvious answers. Preparing children in classrooms means preparing them to solve problems that have not even been invented yet so we need them to be able to approach novel problems and come up with novel solutions. So what question did I ask? I asked her, "How much do you weigh?" I then had her stand on the scale and I handed her the suitcase while I read the scale.

Beyond the Basics

Effective problem solving is essential throughout life and allows students to approach new situations with confidence. To solve a problem is to figure out a way to handle or cope with something that is bothering or puzzling you. Unfortunately, real problem solving is rarely taught in elementary school. "The average fifth grader received five times as much instruction in basic skills as instruction focused on problem solving or reasoning: this ratio was 10:1 in first and third grades" (Pianta, Belsky, Houts, & Morrison, 2007, p. 1795).

This focus on basic skills is reflected in the United States' twenty-sixth rank in math on the 2012 Program for International Student Assessment (PISA, 2012). According to Gurria, who oversees the PISA, U.S. students had a difficult time on the PISA with "tasks that are cognitively demanding and which require complex mathematical thinking" (2013, para. 7). He added that the Common Core State Standards for Mathematics (2010) emphasize these cognitively demanding skills.

Basic skills are important, but they are not enough to meet the requirements of the Common Core mathematical standards, which ask students to use higher-order thinking and communication in mathematics, just as they must do in reading and writing. For example, one of the Common Core Mathematical Practices that applies at all grade levels with increasing complexity is "Construct viable arguments and critique the reasoning of others."

Many early childhood educators are concerned that the Common Core Mathematical Standards are not developmentally appropriate as defined by the National Association for the Education of Young Children (NAEYC). This is a legitimate concern whenever a new set of standards is introduced for mathematics. Jean Piaget demonstrated many years ago quite effectively that young children's reasoning differs from adult reasoning in mathematical logic. Many educational experts agree that the issue is not with the standards; it is more likely that the issue is with the curriculum and testing.

As soon as a new curriculum is introduced, educational companies produce all sorts of new materials that are supposed to meet the new standards. However the materials needed to meet the standards already exist and have been around for a long time. For example, a good set of wooden unit blocks and adequate time to build with them would meet a number of the mathematics standards for kindergarten, and they would also meet the goals of conceptual understanding and application of mathematical ideas.

As for testing, paper and pencil tests or computer administered tests for children are never appropriate for children before grade three. Schools that emphasize testing in grades k-2 are wasting precious time and resources for no purpose as these tests will have little value in understanding what children know about math.

Problem-Solving Process

To meet new cognitively-demanding requirements, students must understand and practice their problem-solving skills frequently. Problem solving may vary from context to context, but we are presenting a five step problem-solving process that can be applied flexibly to most situations. The steps are: (1) identify the problem or question, (2) determine what relevant information is already known, (3) identify method(s) of answering the question or solving the problem, (4) solve the problem or answer the question, and (5) evaluate the solution. The details of the problem-solving process are not as important as students having a deep understanding of a process that allows them to apply their skills to a variety of problems. Students should have opportunities to practice these steps with different types of problems, including those that have multiple answers and those that have no answers or at least no good ones. In order to complete this process, they need to be given more time to complete fewer problems. *Less is more.*

Identify the Problem or Question

Teachers need to demonstrate and encourage students not to jump to solving the problem before they have carefully considered the nature of the problem. They also need to be careful not to solve problems for students without giving them opportunities to solve them themselves. For example, if students are arguing during work time, the teacher might ask each one to calmly state the problem and listen to one another. Once the problem is clearly stated then the teacher can guide them in finding a solution. In science too, students need to identify the question before they make a hypothesis or conduct an experiment.

The same idea applies to mathematical problems; students need to spend time identifying the question before they begin planning the solution. Texas and Jones (2013) ask students to identify the question and then make it into an answer statement and leave a blank for the solution. For example, if the question is "How much change will Jake get back from the cashier?" Students would write, "Jake will get _____ change back" before they even plan how they are going to solve the problem. This process helps students to think about a reasonable answer. Teachers may want students to write down what they already know about the answer, such as that it will be an amount of money.

Determine What Information Is Known

Students need to separate relevant information from information that will not help them solve the problem. In the last example, perhaps Jake went to the store with three friends but that doesn't have anything to do with how much change he should get back from the cashier, so students need to ignore this information. Texas and Jones (2013) recommend that students write down the information that they believe will be important in solving the problem.

In other problems, students may be missing information. For example, the teacher may ask a small group of students to determine the area of the classroom floor. From previous learning, they know that area is determined by length times width but they don't have this information. Next, they have to figure out how they will get this information, such as borrowing a tape-measure from the teacher and measuring the length and width of the classroom. If the classroom is irregularly shaped, they will have to determine how to deal with this. The Bus Schedule activity at the end of the chapter is another problem with missing information.

When students are conducting research on topics during a thematic unit, they need to ask similar questions. What do they already know about the topic? What questions still remain? Where or how could this information be obtained?

Hypotheses in science require students to make educated guesses about the answers to questions based on known facts. Students need to ask themselves what they already know about the question before making a hypothesis about the answer. If they feel they don't have enough information, they may need to do more research before making a hypothesis.

Identify Methods or Strategies to Solve the Problem

The Common Core encourages students to plan out a strategy for solving problems or answering questions rather than just solving the problem immediately. For example, one of the Common Core's essential mathematical practices is "Make sense of problems and persevere in solving them."

There are many possible problem-solving strategies, and teachers need to introduce them slowly. In mathematics, much of the work may involve deciding what type of calculations should be done—adding or subtracting, multiplying or dividing, and so forth. Students may determine that drawings or manipulatives will help them in solving the problem or that they need to use calculators to find the solution. Other problem-solving strategies that could be applied in mathematics as well as other subjects include conducting an experiment, doing a survey, finding patterns, making a chart or other diagram, using the process of elimination, weighing the pros and cons, getting more information, or asking for more expert help.

Some problems don't involve mathematics at all. For example, Jessica needs a new winter jacket. Her mother has agreed to take her shopping after school but she doesn't have much time to go from store to store. What is the best way for Jessica to get a jacket she likes? There are a few possible problem-solving strategies, including asking her friends where they shop for their jackets or searching online and seeing what is in stock at various stores. She may also make a list of what criteria she has for a jacket to make the decision process quicker when she arrives at the store.

During this stage, students come up with an estimate or prediction of a reasonable answer. They will use this to check their answer during the final step.

Solve the Problem

At this point, students apply their selected strategy or strategies to the problem at hand. The Common Core asks them to "attend to precision" while solving the problem. It would be frustrating if students go through all the steps properly only to make an error in their calculations.

Evaluate the Solution

Students should go back to their estimate or prediction. If their answer differs significantly, they should review the process to see if their solution is wrong or their estimate was way off. Students also should learn to check their answers using an alternative solution strategy. In some cases, this may mean using addition to check subtraction or division to check multiplication. In other cases, students may make a chart to check an answer they found using manipulatives or see if their answer fits into a predicted pattern. If they are trying to solve a real-life problem, they also need to consider whether the solution is practical. Students may plan a healthy meal for the class, but it is not practical if it would cost $1,000 to feed the class one healthy meal.

The Process and Problems

Although the problem-solving process has been presented here step-by-step, students may go back and forth between steps before actually solving and successfully checking the problem. For example, they may be trying to solve the problem and realize that they need to collect more information or they may check their solution and decide it doesn't make sense and they need to find another strategy.

At first students should be given well-defined problems with clear solution paths and goals. As they become more proficient in problem solving, they should be asked to provide more than one way to solve the problems. They also need to be given real-life problems that have more than one solution and be asked to evaluate the possible solutions. In addition, in life we are often presented with problems with no solution, such as needing something that is not within our budget. They can then be asked what they could do instead of buying an item that is too expensive for their budget.

Less Is More for Problem Solvers

Less is more can definitely be applied to problem solving. Although students certainly need to learn how to do basic computation, they also need to have opportunities to solve increasingly more difficult problems. In order for them to have time to complete the problem-solving process and do the higher-order thinking required by the Common Core and other standards, students should be given more time for fewer problems than are usually included in elementary school instruction.

All of us have heard the saying, "Practice makes perfect." That saying is often applied in math instruction by giving students numerous practice problems for each new concept. However, brain research now indicates that the type of practice people have with new concepts is more important than the quantity of practice. "It is via deliberate practice and concentration that learning is fostered—and it is more the quality than quantity of study time that is critical" (Hattie, 2012, p. 110).

A boy I was tutoring was required to write his spelling words 10 times each on the principle that the repetition would improve his rote spelling ability. His execution of the task was to write the first letter on each word 10 times, then he would write the second letter and so forth. He had managed to make the task automatic so as to speed up the process and therefore managed to not improve his ability to spell. Clearly asking for even more repetitions would never improve the outcome. So is there a better way?

Spaced Repetitions
The impact of practice can be increased through spaced repetitions and interleaving. Spaced repetition means that concepts are introduced and practiced with a few problems and then

reviewed and practiced again after a considerable interval, such as 30 days. ". . . When we first acquire memories, they are volatile, subject to change or to disappear. Exposing ourselves to information repeatedly over time fixes it more permanently in our minds, by strengthening the representation of the information that is embedded in our neural networks" (Paul, 2013, para. 4). Not only does spaced repetition help people remember more, but it also helps them have a deeper understanding of concepts. "Thus, reviews may do more than simply increase the amount learned: they may shift the learner's attention away from the verbatim details of the material being studied to its deeper conceptual structure" (Dempster, 1991, p. 71).

Interleaved Practice

Interleaved practice, which involves mixing the types of problems in practice sessions, also increases deep conceptual understanding. When a teacher introduces a new concept in math, students are usually given practice problems that involve only that concept so students don't have to think about what process or processes they are going to use to solve the problem. For example, if a teacher just introduced subtraction of fractions, the students know that the practice problems will involve subtracting fractions and they don't have to really think about what the problem is asking them to do. This is one of the reasons that students may be successful on practice problems in class but have difficulty on tests in which a variety of problems are presented and the students have to decide what method(s) should be used to solve the problem. Interleaving or mixing the types of problems forces students to think about what the problem is asking them to do and choose the correct process for solving it. Taylor and Rohrer (2010) conducted a study with fourth graders in which they taught two groups of students how to calculate the number of corners, faces, edges, and angles in a shape if you know the number of base sides. Both groups received the same instruction and the same post-test, but one group had interleaved practice that mixed corner, face, edge, and angle problems while the other group had practice that grouped all the corner problems together, all the face problems together, and so forth. The group that had inter-leaved practice scored twice as well as the other group on the post-test. Thus, it wasn't the number of practice problems that mattered but the order that they were presented.

Most math textbooks are not organized for spaced repetition or interleaving, but teachers can implement these ideas with little extra effort. When concepts are first introduced, only use a few of the practice problems in the book and assign students to do practice problems from concepts that were previously introduced, but were not used at that time. When using ques-tions from quiz or test banks, make sure to mix up problems from recently introduced concepts and problems from concepts that were introduced earlier. After grading the quiz or test, review the answers with students. This provides both spaced repetition and interleaving. Students may do fewer problems, but they will remember the concepts better. When they encounter a new problem, they will have the deep understanding needed to decide what method(s) will help them solve the problem.

Writing and Mathematics

For many years, writing and mathematics were not mentioned in the same sentence let alone the same lesson. Now we know that writing helps people to learn and remember almost any topic better. "When you engage your students in writing tasks as part of your social studies, science, and math instruction, your students will think more about what they are learning: More and higher-level thinking will result in more learning" (Cun-ningham & Allington, 2011, p. 193).

In order to write or even orally discuss mathematics, students need to have a strong grasp of mathematics vocabulary. "Vocabu-lary is the foundation upon which mathematical understandings develop" (Texas & Jones, 2013, p. 27). Mathematical vocabulary can be included in personal dictionaries or vocabulary journals and on Word Walls. Students should be encouraged to draw pictures of the word or phrase, write their own definitions, and provide examples. Teachers should make sure the students understand the special meanings that words have in mathematics, such as "square" and "root" in "square root" or the "volume" of a "cube." These multi-meaning words can be confusing for all students, especially English language learners.

Problem Solving and Integrated Units

Mathematics often needs to be taught separately from integrated units in order to properly introduce new concepts, but mathematical concepts and problem solving can be reinforced through thematic units. One example is the Pulse Rate activity at the end of the chapter that can be integrated into a health unit. Some schools include problem-based units in their curriculum. This helps students understand practical applications of problem solving. Some examples are obesity, water shortages, and cyberbullying.

Problem Solving and Standardized Tests

The mathematical portions of standardized tests, especially those based on the Common Core standards require that students use higher-order thinking skills. It is no longer sufficient for them to memorize mathematical facts or formulas. They need to be able to apply complex problem-solving skills to the problems presented on the test, including being able to analyze what the questions are asking them and being able to choose an appropriate solution strategy. They will gain the confidence necessary to approach different problems when they are given varied problems in class and the time needed to understand the underlying concepts behind them. Students do need some practice with the vocabulary and format of the test, but more real problem solving will prepare them for the tests and life.

Decision Making

Children make decisions every day from an early age and can be assisted in making better decisions with guidance at home and school. Decision making should be presented in context rather than as a separate lesson and can be integrated into almost any area of study. The Missing the Bus activity at the end of the chapter provides a decision-making exercise that can be modified for almost any grade level.

In the early years, teachers can present a simple problem orally and students can learn the steps in the decision-making process. For example, the teacher can say he wants to play a phonics game with them in which they will look for things that begin with a particular sound. He says, "I can't decide if we should play the game inside or outside, and I want your help." He will then assist the students in making a list of reasons to go outside, and he will write them on the board or chart paper. For example, "we don't go out much so it would be fun to go outside" or "we can find new things outside." Then he could ask the students about reasons not to go outside and write these down too. For example, "it is cold outside" or "we might not find enough things in the fenced-in area." After this activity is completed and pros and cons are reread together, students can vote on whether or not to go outside.

Decision Making and Literature

Decision-making lessons also can be integrated with literature. In most fictional literature, the characters are presented with a problem that they have to solve. The teacher can read aloud to students until the problem is presented and then stop to allow students to discuss or write about what they would do if they were the character(s) facing the problem. The class should do this together the first couple of times, and later students can work with partners or small groups to repeat the process. First students should identify the problem and the character's goal. Then students should explore possible solutions to the problem, explaining why they think the solution would be effective. Finally, ask students what they think would happen next if the character chose their solution. Older students can be challenged to come up with more than one way the problem could be resolved and to evaluate the pros and cons of each possible solution.

Decision Making and Behavior Lessons

Often, decision making is integrated with lessons on behavior issues, such as not talking to strangers, bullying, or drinking alcohol. Rather than simply telling students not to do these things, present them with scenarios that are appropriate to their age and ask them what they might do. For example, younger students might be asked what they would do if a stranger approached them and asked for their help looking for a lost pet or if someone came to pick them up at school that they didn't recognize. Older students might be asked what they would do if some of their friends were bullying someone else they all knew. Teachers should be careful not to make decisions for students unless there is an immediate danger. When appropriate, they should seek help from students about decisions concerning everything from bulletin boards to classroom management.

Planning

Planning, another important life skill, is an extension of problem solving. A common complaint of employers is that employees don't think ahead or plan for the future. As a result supplies and equipment are not ordered in time, meetings are scheduled too close together, or reports are not completed early enough to allow for revisions and editing. A perpetually late employee tells his boss, "Well I got stuck in traffic." To which the boss replies, "Then how did I manage to get here on time?" Teachers can help even young students understand the planning process. Planning can begin as a whole class activity and be integrated into thematic units. For example, teachers can have students help plan for a healthy snack during a nutrition unit, plan to invite a speaker to talk on a topic being studied in class, or plan what they will need to do to test a hypothesis in science.

One class wanted to invite families to hear them perform a Reader's Theater that they had been practicing. The teacher guided the students in deciding when they would have the performance, where they would do the performance, how families would be invited, what materials would be needed, and what permission they would need to do the performance. For example, they decided the classroom was too small for the performance and the families so they had to get permission to use the cafetorium when it wasn't being used for meals or other activities. They decided to make their own invitations for the event and ask the families to bring snacks to share. The students soon learned that there are many steps involved in planning an event. They even planned the clean-up after the event.

Conclusion

Students should have opportunities to solve problems, make decisions, and plan. By doing fewer problems, students can focus on the process of problem solving. Instruction should move away from rote practice or memorization and into deeper understanding of the underlying concepts of mathematics. The following are examples of how teachers can help students learn and practice problem solving, decision making, and planning.

Sample Lessons

Missing the Bus

Purpose: To guide students in solving a real-life problem and evaluating the strengths and weaknesses of different proposed solutions.

Participants: Kindergarten through fifth-grade students

Preparation: Construct a scenario appropriate for the grade level of the students. Teachers may want to include times in the scenario to encourage mathematical thinking, as well as other problem-solving skills for appropriate grade levels.

Sample Scenario: It was only October and James had missed the bus three times this year. His mother and father were angry with him because they didn't have time to take him to school without being late to work themselves. The bus came to the corner near his house at 7:45 am. His alarm clock went off at 6:45 am but sometimes he hit the snooze button and it was 7:00 before he got up. It took him about 20 minutes to take a shower, brush his teeth and hair, and get dressed. It took him 15 minutes to eat breakfast and put his dishes in the sink. He also needed to make sure the dog had food and water before leaving for school, which took about five minutes. He needed to leave a few minutes to put on his jacket, get his backpack organized, and walk to the corner. The problem was that he shared the bathroom with his brother and sister. When he got up, his sister was usually in the bathroom for 20 minutes so he had to wait to take his shower. How much time did James have to get ready if he got up at 6:45 am? At 7:00 am? How much time did it take him to get ready if he didn't have to wait for the bathroom? Does he have enough time? What are some ways that James could make sure he didn't miss the bus?

Activity Description

1. Present the scenario to students. Make sure they can see it projected or have it on a printed copy throughout the process.
2. Have students do the mathematical calculations if appropriate.
3. Have students work with partners to come up with possible solutions and write them down if age appropriate.
4. Discuss the solutions with the class. If there are only a couple of solutions, encourage students to think of more. For example, James could take a shower at night rather than in the morning. He could eat breakfast and feed the dog while his sister was in the bathroom.
5. Choose one or more of the proposed solutions. If this is a new process for students, analyze the solutions for strengths and weaknesses together. Or have students work with partners to analyze the strengths and weaknesses of different proposed solutions.
6. Discuss the possible solutions with the students and decide which one or combination of solutions would work best.

Common Core Mathematical Practices: Reason abstractly and quantitatively. Construct viable arguments and critique the reasoning of others.

Pulse Rate

Purpose: To engage students with authentic mathematical problem solving. To integrate math into a health thematic unit.

Participants: Third- through fifth-grade students

Preparation: Students will need to know how to multiply two digit numbers by two before being able to complete this assignment.

Activity Description
1. Teach students how to take their pulse.
2. Have students take their pulse for 30 seconds and record the number.
3. Have students run in place for five minutes and quickly take their pulse for 30 seconds again.
4. Record the second pulse rate.
5. Explain to students that pulse rates are usually reported in beats per minute. Ask the students to calculate their before and after pulse rates for a minute and record those numbers.
6. Ask students to calculate the difference between their before running and after running pulse rates. Ask them to assess the reasonableness of their answer.
7. Discuss why pulse rates are important to know, especially for an exercise regime.

Common Core Mathematical Standard 3, 8: Solve two-step word problems using the four operations. Assess the reasonableness of answers using mental computation and estimation strategies including rounding.

Bus Schedule

Purpose: To help students understand reading charts, patterns, and completing patterns.

Participants: Third- through fifth-grade students

Preparation: Copy the city bus schedule in Table 4.1 or create your own bus schedule with local streets. Remove some of the times so students can determine the patterns.

Student Problem: Rudy lives near the 10th St. bus stop and his grand-mother lives near the 76th St. bus stop. On Saturday, he wants to get to his grandmother's at about 11:30 am but part of the bus schedule is missing. What time should Rudy leave if he wants to get to his grand-mother's at about 11:30 pm? (10:34) What time would he get to her stop if he took the bus that came to his bus stop at 9:04? (9:42) What time would he get there if he took the bus that came to his bus stop at 10:34? (11:12) What time would he get there if he took the bus that left at 12:04? (12:42) How do you know? (Several ways to figure out the missing information.)

Modification: Teachers could have students practice answering questions with completed parts of the chart and help students discover the pat-tern in the chart before working with the missing part of the chart.

Common Core Mathematics Standards: Represent and Interpret Data

Mathematical Practices: Look for and express regularity in repeated reasoning.

TABLE 4.1 Bus Schedule

Daily	2nd St.	10th St.	20th St.	35th St.	44th St.	60th St.	76th St.	82nd St.
	6:30 am	6:34	6:39	6:49	6:56	7:04	7:12	7:17
	7 am	7:04	7:09	7:19	7:26	7:34	7:42	7:47
	7:30 am	7:34	7:39	7:49	7:56	8:04	8:12	8:17
	8 am	8:04	8:09	8:19	8:26	8:34	8:42	8:47
	9 am	9:04	9:09	9:19	9:26	9:34	9:42	9:47
	10:30 am	10:34	10:39	10:49	10:56			
	12 pm	12:04	12:09	12:19	12:26			

References

Common Core State Standards for Mathematics (2010). National Governors Association Center for Best Practices, Council of Chief State School Officers. Retrieved from www.corestandards.org/the-standards

Cunningham, P. M., & Allington, R. L. (2011). *Classrooms that work: They can all read and write* (5th ed.). Boston, MA: Pearson.

Dempster, F. N. (1991). Synthesis of research on reviews and tests. *Educational Leadership, 48*(7), 71–76. Retrieved from www.ascd.org/ASCD/pdf/journals/ed_lead/el_199104_dempster.pdf

Gurria, A. (2013, December 3). A USA and international perspective on 2012 PISA results. Retrieved from www.oecd.org/unitedstates/a-usa-and-international-perspective-on-2012-pisa-results.htm

Hattie, J. (2012). *Visible learning for teachers: Maximizing impact on learning*. New York, NY: Routledge.

Paul, A. M. (2013, September). When homework is a waste of time. *Time Magazine*. Retrieved from http://ideas.time.com/2013/09/05/when-homework-is-a-waste-of-time/

Pianta, R. C., Belsky, J., Houts, R., & Morrison, F. (2007). Opportunities to learn in America's elementary classrooms. *Science, 315*(30), 1795–1796.

The Program for International Student Assessment (PISA, 2012). National Center for Education Statistics, Institute of Education Sciences. Retrieved from http://nces.ed.gov/surveys/pisa/

Taylor, K., & Rohrer, D. (2010). The effects of interleaved practice. *Applied Cognitive Psychology, 24*, 837–848.

Texas, L. A., & Jones, T. L. (2013). *Strategies for Common Core mathematics: Implementing the standards for mathematical practice K-5*. Larchmont, NY: Eye on Education.

Weimer, M. (2010, August 31). To improve students' problem solving skills add group work to the equation. Retrieved from www.facultyfocus.com/articles/teaching-and-learning/to-improve-students-problem-solving-skills-add-group-work-to-the-equation/

Other Resource

National Council of Teacher of Mathematics. www.nctm.org/Default.aspx

5

Effective Communicators

The two words "information" and "communication" are often used interchangeably, but they signify quite different things. Information is giving out; communication is getting through.

Sydney J. Harris

Scenario
Writer's Workshop vs. Test Preparation

Mr. Lopez, a fourth-grade teacher, just finished with a week of professional development on Writer's Workshop in July and really wanted to implement it with his class during the next school year. He felt the workshop format fit in well with the *less is more* ideas that his school had adopted the previous year. Students would write fewer but longer essays. They would have opportunities to brainstorm, draft, revise, edit, and publish some of their work over days or even weeks instead of just writing a new short draft every couple of days. They would be able to choose their own topics instead of always responding to teacher-made prompts. Writing strategies, grammar, and other lessons that had previously been taught through worksheets would be demonstrated by him during daily mini-lessons and practiced by the students during real writing and peer-revising and editing. As students were writing, he would conference with them individually about the next steps they could take to improve their writing.

Despite all the positive aspects of Writer's Workshop, Mr. Lopez wondered if it would prepare his students for writing on the state standardized exam at the end of the year. In contrast to Writer's Workshop, testing situations give students prompts to write about rather than free choice of topics, prescribe a format such as a persuasive letter, limit time to complete drafts without much opportunity to revise or edit, and prevent students from seeking help from other people or other resources. He did some research on the Internet and found out how other teachers were taking advantage of the benefits of Writer's Workshop and still preparing their students for standardized writing tests at the end of the year.

Combining Writer's Workshop and Test Preparation

Many teachers like Mr. Lopez feel that Writer's Workshop prepares students for real-life writing in which texts must be revised and edited before they are presented to other people. They like the idea of being able to provide students with feedback while they are writing so they can improve their writing immediately rather than waiting until they receive a graded paper several days after they completed it. Yet they are concerned about how to combine Writer's Workshop with preparing students for writing to prompts in a specific format on end of the year tests.

Researchers have studied classrooms in which teachers have successfully combined the benefits of Writers Workshop with the realities of test preparation (Wolf & Wolf, 2002; Wollman-Bonilla, 2004). Although the details in the third through seventh-grade classrooms differed, similar instructional patterns emerged. All of the classrooms used a Writer's Workshop type of format to be able to provide the time and feedback needed to improve the quality of their students' writing. They also used mentor text as models of specific types of writing. (See the activity on Figurative Language through Mentor Texts at the end of the chapter.) However, unlike strict Writer's Workshop, students in these classrooms were sometimes given required topics and formats for their writing. The teacher provided sample text and mini-lessons that correlated with the variety of genres that were expected on the state writing test and then students followed that example.

These exemplary writing teachers taught their students about the rubrics that were used to evaluate writing in their states. They provided students with examples of writing that had been assessed using these rubrics and discussed with them why the examples received specific scores. Students then learned to apply these same rubrics during self- and peer-revision and editing sessions. The teachers wanted students to understand how their own writing samples could be improved. "The point is not to wrench a piece in line with standardized rubric criteria, but to meet and then push beyond the boundaries of established rubrics to take writing to the next level" (Wolf & Wolf, 2002, p. 232).

Students who learn to write well throughout the school year still need *occasional* practice with the format and limitations of testing situations. Teachers in the research studies tried to simulate the testing situation as closely as possible by giving students test-like prompts, limiting time, and not allowing students to talk to each other or use resources that would not be available during the test in these practice sessions.

Although these studies were conducted prior to the Common Core (2010), similar instructional strategies can be used to meet the Common Core standards, prepare students for testing situations, and prepare them for lifelong writing. The Common Core requires students to become proficient in writing narrative, argument, and informational texts. The Persuasive Letter Writing activity at the end of the chapter is an example of teaching argument writing. If teachers always allow students to choose the topic and type of writing they will do during Writer's Workshop, some may never learn all three types of writing. At times, teachers should set specific goals for student's writing, such as informational reports tied to the current integrated unit. Then they can teach students how to write informational reports through the Writer's Workshop format, including sharing exemplary texts, mini-lessons, and regular feedback throughout the writing process.

As teachers work to combine good writing instruction and test preparation, they should remember *less is more*. When this approach is used, students will probably write fewer pieces but they will revise, edit, and share some of their writing, which often does not happen if teachers only prepare students for writing on tests.

Writing and Technology

If students are really going to learn to revise for content and edit for grammar, spelling, and punctuation, they must have regular access to computers. Research indicates that the use of word processors for writing improves the length and quality of the texts compared to paper and pencil writing (Merchant, 2008). Not surprisingly, students also make more revisions (additions, deletions, replacements, and moving text) when using a word processor because the process is so much easier than having to copy over a whole paper by hand in order to make revisions. Word processors can support editing for grammar and spelling, but students need to be taught how to use these tools. For example, if the spell checker indicates that a word is incorrect, they should check to be sure that it is not a proper noun or other word that is not included in the word-processing dictionary. Finally, they should read their work aloud to themselves to hear the flow of the work and catch grammar or other errors that may have been missed previously. (Some suggestions for funding technology are found in Chapter 12.)

Grammar and Spelling

Although almost everyone agrees that grammar and spelling are important, when and how to teach them is a hot topic of debate. If teachers place too much emphasis on grammar, punctuation, and spelling (mechanics) in writing from the beginning, many students will be reluctant to write. Their writing will be short and stilted because they will only use words that they think are spelled correctly. They also will be constantly asking for teacher feedback on their spelling and grammar during independent writing time, which detracts from the content of the writing and requires tremendous teacher time. If spelling and grammar are never emphasized, students begin to assume they are not important.

There are several ways teachers approach this challenge. The emphasis during the first draft of writing always should be on content, but when students begin to edit their own work and do peer-editing, mini-lessons can focus on grammar and spelling with increasing difficulty. For example, at the beginning, students may be asked to check their writing to make sure there is ending punctuation for every sentence. When most students have mastered this task they may move on to commas in series of words or phrases and so forth. Students will have a checklist for editing that is updated throughout the year as new concepts are added. If this process begins in the early grades, teachers can work on more difficult concepts, such as subject-verb agreement in the upper grades after a brief review of the easier concepts. In addition to mini-lessons, self-editing, and peer-editing, teachers can take advantage of individual writing conferences to explain a few of the corrections that they have made on students' work to prepare it for publishing. Teachers also can give students examples of their own writing or writing from previous students with names removed to give them extra practice with editing. Sometimes the teacher may show edits on the papers and guide students to explain why those edits were made.

The best way to improve spelling is to read the word spelled correctly in text. Reading the word repeatedly in text reinforces the brain's pattern matching ability. Studies have shown that reading incorrectly spelled words leads to the brain questioning itself as to what is the correct spelling. So to become a better speller, read.

Keeping with *less is more,* teachers should use fewer grammar worksheets and weekly spelling tests because there is little evidence that students apply what they learn on these during actual writing. Instead teachers should encourage students to edit their own and peer's writing for grammar and spelling as is grade appropriate. They should also encourage wide reading so that students repeatedly see words spelled correctly and grammar used properly.

Writing across the Curriculum

One of the advantages of teaching through integrated units, as is recommended in this book, is that students have opportunities to write throughout the day, not just during a specified writing time. They learn that writing can be used for many purposes, such as brainstorming, taking notes, making lists to remember things, and communicating with others. Not only does practice with writing throughout the curriculum help students become more proficient writers, it also helps them think more deeply about social studies, science, math, and other subject areas (Cunningham & Allington, 2011). There are many ways to incorporate writing across the curriculum including quick writes, journals, graphic organizers, and sticky notes.

Oral Language across the Curriculum

Less is more applies to oral language development too. Put simply, teachers should talk less and let students talk more if they want to develop students' speaking and listening skills. Students need to have many opportunities to listen and speak for a variety of reasons throughout the school day. The Guessing Games at the end of the chapter are examples of speaking and listening games. When children are asked to remain quiet, even in the cafeteria, they don't have opportunities to use their listening and speaking skills for reasons relevant to them. When almost all class instruction is completed as a whole group, only the teacher and one student at a time have opportunities to speak. Very often a few students dominate the talking while the rest of the class remains quiet.

Therefore, one of the most effective ways to develop listening and speaking skills is to have students work in pairs or small groups in which students have many opportunities to listen and speak. (Chapter 7 provides more ideas for student collaboration.) Reluctant students will be more likely to speak with a partner or in a small group than during whole class instruction. Teachers can structure these activities to encourage everyone to participate by providing activities with open-ended questions related to the current integrated unit. For example, the teacher might lead a small group discussion in which students are asked what they think it would be like to live without electricity as part of a history lesson. Each student in the small group can be encouraged to respond and the teacher can ask questions to help the students expand on their answers. The teacher can also use academic language, such as "challenges" or "imagine," to help students expand their vocabulary. Listening and speaking skills can be applied across the curriculum. For instance, a small student-led group could be asked to come up with as many equations as possible with the answer "24," and each student would say and write their equation as one paper is passed around the group.

In order to communicate effectively, students also need to learn to take turns talking and listening. They should learn to respond to what the other person is saying appropriately and ask questions to clarify meaning. These characteristics of effective listening and speaking are reflected in the Common Core anchor standards. For instance the first listening and speaking standard says, "Prepare for and participate effectively in a range of conversations and collaborations with diverse partners, building on others' ideas and expressing their own clearly and persuasively."

Less Is More for Effective Communicators

Rather than having students write a new draft every day or two, teachers should give students the time necessary to develop some of their drafts into more polished papers through revision and editing. Less time should be spent in whole group instruction and more in pairs and small groups so that students have more opportunities to listen and speak. Effective communication instruction helps students learn to listen, speak, and write. It also helps students to think more deeply about topics and organize their ideas. The ability to communicate with others about a variety of topics is inextricably linked to critical thinking and learning. The following are examples of ways that teachers can apply *less is more* to implement high-quality communication instruction in their classrooms.

Sample Lessons

Guessing Games

Participants: Kindergarten through fifth-grade students

Purpose: To develop listening and vocabulary skills

Preparation: Place students in teams of three or four. Come up with a list of things related to the current thematic unit, such as different animals or different forms of government.

Activity Description

1. Tell students that they are going to play a guessing game related to the current thematic unit. The teacher is going to think of something related to the unit and they have to ask yes or no questions to determine what it is.
2. Explain the rules to the students. The teacher will call on a team to ask a question that can be answered with a yes or no. For example, "Does the animal have fur?" If no other team has asked the question before, they get a point and the teacher answers the question.
3. After the class correctly guesses what the teacher was thinking, the team with the most points gets to be the teacher. The teacher can just tell them what item to think about or let them choose from previously determined items that have been written on slips of paper and placed in a paper bag.

Notes: This is a good game to play as an integrated unit review for 15 or 20 minutes. Kindergartners and some first graders may need more modeling of how to ask questions or they will simply guess one thing after another rather than using a process of elimination. Once students understand how to play the game, they can play themselves in small groups or at centers. The teacher may want to provide them with picture cards or index cards with different choices written on them. A similar game can be played in which one student describes the item on the picture card or index card and the other students in the small group try to guess what he is describing.

Common Core Language Anchor 3: Apply knowledge of language to understand how language functions in different contexts, to make effective choices for meaning or style, and to comprehend more fully when reading and listening.

Common Core Speaking and Listening Anchor 2: Integrate and evaluate information presented in diverse media and formats, including visually, quantitatively, and orally.

Figurative Language through Mentor Texts

Participants: First through fifth-grade students

Purpose: To use mentor text to demonstrate the use of figurative language. To have students use the mentor text as a model for their own writing.

Preparation: Choose a book with figurative language. Some examples are: *Quick as a Cricket* (Wood, 1990) and *Crazy Like a Fox: A Simile Story* (Leedy, 2009).

Activity Description
1. Read the book with figurative language to the students.
2. Discuss some examples from the book. For example, young children may think that saying someone is "quick as a cricket" means that they are a cricket.
3. The students should then help the teacher write some similes about him, which will be displayed on the board.
4. Have students write similes about themselves. Young children can just write one simile and illustrate it. Upper elementary

students could write a short picture book using the mentor text as a model.

5. Share the writing on bulletin boards or with other students. If two grade levels are doing cross-aged tutoring, this would be a good project to share.

Notes: Mentor texts are also a good way to help students understand metaphors and idioms.

Common Core Language Anchor 5: Demonstrate understanding of figurative language, word relationships, and nuances in word meanings.

Persuasive Letter Writing

Participants: Fourth through fifth-grade students

Purpose: To help students research and write opinion pieces supported by evidence.

Preparation: Make sure that students understand the format of a letter. Provide students with examples of effective persuasive letters. During a mini-lesson point out how the opinion pieces support their reasoning.

Activity Description
1. Brainstorm topics of interest to students as a class. For example, the food in the cafeteria, the lack of computers in the classroom, or the beginning and ending time of school.
2. Have students choose one of the topics that was brainstormed or another one of interest to them and write an opinion statement, such as "students should be allowed to bring cell phones to school."
3. Next have students come up with at least three reasons they believe that statement is true.
4. Ask them what research they will need to do to find evidence to support their reasoning. For example, if they say cell phones

promote safety at school then this statement needs to be supported with facts.

5. Give students an opportunity to do research and to write their letters over several days with teacher support.
6. Have students revise and edit their letters with partners.
7. Correct the letters with the student and help them publish the piece in final form.
8. Send the letters to appropriate leaders.

Common Core Writing Anchor 1: Write arguments to support claims in an analysis of substantive topics or texts using valid reasoning and relevant and sufficient evidence.

Writing Anchor 9: Draw evidence from literary or informational texts to support analysis, reflection, and research.

References

Common Core State Standards (2010). National Governors Association Center for Best Practices, Council of Chief State School Officers. Retrieved from www.corestandards.org/the-standards

Cunningham, P. M., & Allington, R. L. (2011). *Classrooms that work: They can all read and write* (5th ed.). Boston, MA: Pearson.

Leedy, L. (2009). *Crazy like a fox: A simile story.* New York, NY: Holiday House.

Merchant, G. (2008). Digital writing in the early years. In J. Coiro, M. Knobel, C. Lankshear, & D. J. Leu (Eds.), *Handbook of research on new literacies* (p. 751–774). New York, NY: Lawrence Erlbaum Associates.

Wolf, S. A., & Wolf, K. P. (2002). Teaching *true* and *to* the test in writing. *Language Arts, 79*(3), 229–240.

Wollman-Bonilla, J. E. (2004). Principled teaching to(wards) the test? Persuasive writing in two classrooms. *Language Arts, 81*(6), 502–511.

Wood, A. (1990). *Quick as a cricket.* Wiltshire, England: Child's Play International Ltd.

Other Resources

International Reading Association. www.reading.org
National Council of Teachers of English. www.ncte.org
Reading and Writing. www.readwritethink.org
The Reading and Writing Project. www.readingandwritingproject.com
Writing. http://elemed.ucps.k12.nc.us/writing/LaunchingPacket%20
    2007.pdf
Writer's Workshop. http://busyteacherscafe.com/literacy/writing_
    workshop.html

6

Engaged Learners

... the point is that young people who have discovered their passion are far more likely to have the will and discipline to learn and do the difficult things that school and work often require.

Wagner, 2008, p. 205–206

Scenario
Finding the Excitement

Mr. Calvin has been teaching for 15 years and remembers when he was able to excite even reluctant students. He would teach history through drama, science through experiments, and read novels aloud to the students daily with the students begging him to read "just one more chapter." Lately, it didn't seem like he had time to do the things that excited his students and himself about learning. There was too much material to cover and too much time was devoted to preparing for high-stakes tests.

If he didn't help students become excited about learning in elementary school, he was afraid that some of them would be turned off to school and learning for life. He had to figure out ways to prepare students for the high-stakes exams and still be able to engage them in their learning.

Engaging Students

By doing less but doing it better, educators can encourage student engagement and passion. Students who are engaged with their learning spend more time on task, create fewer discipline problems, learn more, and achieve at higher rates. Grit, which is related to intrinsic motivation, is a better predictor of future success than standardized tests (Perkins-Gough & Duckworth, 2013). If we give students more autonomy over their learning, give them opportunities to master new knowledge and skills and give them a purpose for doing so, we will find that they are more likely to be engaged learners.

Research indicates that integrated curriculum is more engaging for students than teaching each subject separately. However, this doesn't simply happen by integrating topics if everything else stays the same. This isn't about teaching fun and exciting activities with no academic purpose either. We suggest six main strategies for building intrinsic motivation through integrated curriculum. They are providing students with 1) real success, 2) appropriate work, 3) relevant assignments, 4) choice, 5) peer and teacher support, and 6) movement and breaks.

Real Success

Students need to feel the joy of true success, of accomplishing something that is important to them. If students do not experience success often, they are less likely to accept challenges or persevere in the face of difficulties. People get satisfaction from getting better at things (Pink, 2011). We learn new cooking or gardening techniques. We do not get paid for these weekend activities; we do them because they are fun and we feel better when we get better at these skills. Schooling is constant attempts to become better at all sorts of activities. Children are intrinsically rewarded when they experience success. Watching a first grader figure out reading is an amazing thing. Once they start to get going, it is often hard to get them to stop reading. Children lose that sense of success when we use a curriculum and assessment system that is punitive.

This is not an advocacy of not keeping score in sports. Feeling true success is facing a tough challenge and overcoming it.

My cooking does not improve if my family rewards me for bringing a frozen pizza home and throwing it into the oven. (Although for some cooks I know that might be a challenge.) On the other hand, seeing a cooking show and trying out a new recipe and having my family enjoy it will encourage me to improve.

To help students experience more success, students need more feedback. In an effort not to hurt students' self esteem, teachers often compliment students for mediocre work, but when students are individually assessed, they do poorly and realize the teacher's words were hollow. Teachers may also use catch phrases, such as "good job," which do not let students know specifically what they are doing well. When students are given specific and accurate feedback either in writing or private conversation, they develop self-knowledge and the ability to evaluate their own work. Providing individual feedback to students requires time, another reason that it is important to do less, but take the time necessary to do it well.

Appropriate Work

In order for students to be successful, they need to have appropriate work. When work is too easy, students become bored and lose interest. They don't learn that everyone has to struggle at times to achieve success. If work is too difficult, students become frustrated and give up, believing they can never succeed. The area between boredom and frustration, the Zone of Proximal Development, is the area in which students develop the most (Gallimore & Tharp, 1990).

In order to design appropriate instruction for individual students, teachers need to know the students' levels of prior knowledge and their predispositions to learning. ". . . knowing prior achievement means not only recognizing the cognitive performance of students, but also their ways and levels of thinking, and their resilience and other self-attributes . . ." (Hattie, 2012, p. 66). Although it may not be possible to create tasks with the appropriate challenge for each student all day long, it is important that they work in their own Zone of Proximal Development some time during the day. The Biographies activity at the end of the chapter is an example of providing appropriate work for all students in the class.

One fourth-grade teacher was told that she taught fourth grade and, therefore, should only be using fourth-grade materials with her students. However, not all students will grow during the year if they only work in fourth-grade materials. She was particularly concerned with students who were only reading at a first- or second-grade level. We can compare it to a high jump. Let's suppose that I can jump 36 inches. With some instruction, I probably could jump a bar at 37 or 38 inches and then higher with more practice, but if the bar was suddenly lifted to 50 inches without incremental increases, I probably would keep knocking the bar down and eventually give up. This is what happens when we as educators do not begin where the student is at.

At the other end of the spectrum, students who always succeed at their work may not develop the grit needed for lifelong learning and success (Perkins-Gough & Duckworth, 2013). Although one might assume that talented students have grit, in reality, they often do not know how to struggle and persevere in the face of the obstacles they are sure to face in life. This is why it is important for all students to work in their own Zone of Proximal Development some time during the day.

Providing appropriate work to this generation also means considering the impact of technology on today's young people (Wagner, 2008). They are sometimes referred to as the Net Generation, but the influence of technology goes well beyond the Internet. From an early age, this generation has been exposed to game consoles, cell phones, tablets, computers, and other technological devices. The big difference between these devices and the television and videos of the last generation is that today's technology is interactive. Students don't just watch and listen; they play games, text messages, and find and share information, music, pictures, and videos that interest them. Providing opportunities for active learning has never been more important than with this generation. They don't want to be passive recipients of knowledge; they want to interact with information and other people. Yet, research indicates that elementary school students spend more than 90 percent of their time in whole group activities or individual seatwork with less than 8 percent of their time being devoted to small group work (Pianta, Belsky, Houts, & Morrison, 2007).

Educators can provide opportunities for active learning in many ways. For example, students can work with partners or small groups and they can choose topics within an integrated unit to research. In addition, students can demonstrate their knowledge through a variety of means, including song, drama, art, videos, and PowerPoint presentations.

Relevant Activities

Work also needs to be relevant to students. Many times students do not understand why they need to learn or do something and consequently are not motivated. There are many ways to make work more relevant for students. For example, teachers can use weather, news events, or other familiar topics to teach a variety of subjects. The Common Core requires kindergartners to describe "familiar people, places, things, and events and, with prompting and support, provide additional details." For older students, sports offer many opportunities for mathematical learning from how batting averages are calculated in baseball to win/ loss percentages for favorite teams. Educators can also make connections between what is being learned at school and their home or community so students can see the importance of what they are learning. For example, the Common Core requires second graders to learn to measure objects. Once students have learned to measure items at school, they can be given a laminated ruler to take home and measure various items, such as the width of a door or the height of their bed.

The essence of providing relevant activities is helping students understand why they are being asked to do something and how it relates to their life. Students know learning is important, but when the curriculum primarily consists of test preparation, they lose interest. A Texas student recently was suspended from school for writing "yolo" (you only live once) on his state exam, and then taking a picture of it with his phone. The test was a practice exam to field test the new exam so it was not being used as a form of evaluation for the student (Nicholson, 2013).The student did not see any relevance or purpose in putting effort into the exam.

Choice

Providing students with more choices is another way to offer appropriate and relevant work. When students have choices, they generally will choose assignments that interest them and are at their level. If they are interested enough in the topic, they may even reach beyond their comfort zone. Most people are more motivated to work hard when they have a choice in the activity. We are not suggesting that students should have complete control of their learning because they do not understand what may be important to them later in life. However, giving students some choices can increase their engagement and productivity.

For example, a fifth-grade teacher may discuss various structural aspects of text, such as chronology, cause/effect, and problem/solution as required by the Common Core and state standards. Then students can choose an appropriate text to read and decide which text structure is used in that text. All the students are working on the same objective but they are applying it to self-selected text. This type of assignment also helps students who are working above or below grade level.

When students are asked to present information to the class, they may be given choices on how to present. The fourth-grade Common Core standards call for students to "add audio recordings and visual displays to presentations when appropriate . . ." These types of presentations will take longer to prepare and present but give students an opportunity to delve more deeply into topics and show their knowledge in creative ways, again supporting the idea that *less is more.*

We often hear that giving students choices does not prepare them for the work world, but Pink (2011) disagrees. Many innovative corporations now are offering workers some time during the week to do whatever they want related to their company. Pink suggests that once people's basic salary level needs are met, they are more motivated to work when they have the opportunity to choose what to work on. Teachers inherently understand this as most teachers that I know work long hours without an expectation of any additional monetary reward. On the other hand, incentive and merit programs have been found to be counterproductive, lead to lower morale, and often lead to negative results like cheating (Lavy, 2007).

Peer and Teacher Support

Students need support from the teacher and their peers if they are going to succeed with challenging work. Students need to know that their efforts will be supported even when they admit they don't understand something or they ask for help. We all make errors and we can use those errors to help us progress. People will try new things and expand their knowledge when they know that they will not be punished, ridiculed, or teased for mistakes. "A positive, caring, respectful climate in the classroom is a prior condition to learning" (Hattie, 2012, p. 70).

Younger students usually want support from the teacher but as students grow older, peer support becomes more and more powerful. The Common Core writing standards from second grade on up require students to work with each other to revise and edit their work. Therefore, it is important for the teacher to model the way to give feedback to other students. For example, the teacher can display his writing for the class to see and have them make constructive suggestions on how it could be improved. The teacher can explain that it is an effort to improve the work and that he does not take the suggestions personally.

Having students work in pairs or groups also encourages more students to be engaged. (Chapter 7 offers ideas for student collaboration.) When the teacher or one student at a time is speaking, it is easy for students to lose interest even if they are sitting quietly. Harris (2013), an expert on student engagement, says that the people in the classroom who are doing the most talking are the ones who are doing the most learning. Unfortunately, in most classrooms, this means that the teacher and a handful of students are doing most of the learning. When students are working in pairs or small groups and the teacher is walking around the room, monitoring students' work and asking questions, many more students will be engaged and motivated. See the Book Sharing activity at the end of the chapter for ideas on how peer sharing can get students excited about reading.

Movement and Taking Breaks

Research has found that learners of all ages are more alert, learn more, and remember more when they are both physically and mentally engaged (Jensen, 2000), yet recess and physical education have been reduced in most elementary schools. Even lunchtime has been cut to 20 or 30 minutes. Therefore, it is important to integrate some movement into instruction. Students can move from one station or center to another, the teacher can post open-ended questions around the room and students can move in small groups to provide answers, or students can pantomime vocabulary words while others guess the word. See the Simon Says Variation at the end of the chapter for another idea to integrate movement into instruction.

Time on task research suggests that the more time children spend on a task, the more they are going to learn. Certainly much research has been done on this topic and, yes, time on task does have an impact on the amount learned. However, there are limits to the amount of time someone can maintain concentration.

Even the business world has found that workers are more productive and safer at their jobs when they have regular breaks. Fifty years ago, recess was an assumed and normal part of the school day. Over the last few decades however, recess time has declined for children and in some cases been eliminated altogether. Ohanian (2002) wrote about how increases in curriculum content requirements and an emphasis on standardized testing were leading to schools eliminating recess from the school day. Even recently the Centers for Disease Control have found that less than 60 percent of elementary schools require regular recess. Only one in eight school districts require recess for all grade levels (Lee et al., 2012). Taking breaks and actually spending less time on task seems counterintuitive, but overall students who get regular breaks and recess do better on classroom work than students who do not get regular breaks.

Self-Regulated Learners

One spring I observed bilingual kindergartners going to centers while the teacher worked with a small group of students on one side of the room. A group of five was at the classroom library center. One of the students was reading a Spanish children's book aloud to the other students, turning it around like the teacher did to show the pictures. After accurately reading each page in Spanish, she correctly translated it into English.

This kindergartner was an example of a highly-motivated, self-regulated learner. Self-regulated learners are ones who are able to set their own realistic goals and monitor and evaluate their own learning. They develop grit, a sense of passion, and perseverance in the pursuit of goals over the long-term. If students are to become independent, lifelong learners, they must learn to regulate their own learning rather than being dependent on teacher directives or peer feedback. Teachers can help to create environments and opportunities that encourage self-regulation.

Student Discussions

First, students must have opportunities for meaningful discussion or dialogue with both the teacher and other students. Research indicates that the great majority of classrooms are dominated by teacher talk and students answering questions with only one acceptable answer. Hattie (2012) writes, "One of the difficulties of so much teacher talk is that it demonstrates to students that teachers are the owners of subject content, and controllers of the pacing and sequencing of learning, and it reduces the opportunities for students to impose their own prior achievement, understanding, sequencing, and questions" (p. 82). Students can only regulate their own learning if they are active participants in the process.

Clear Criteria for Success

Teachers can help students become more self-regulated learners by making the goals of lessons and the criteria for success clear to students. Too often students have no idea of the teacher's expectations. (We have all studied for a test and focused on the wrong things.) Rubrics or examples of successful and unsuccessful work from previous years with names removed help students to understand the teacher's expectations.

Even if students are not at the same level as others in the class, they need to see how they are progressing and what still needs improvement. Runners do not just look at their win and loss records against other runners, they also look to see if their own time is improving at specific distances. Writing instruction provides a particularly good vehicle for this type of self-evaluation. Keeping a portfolio, as discussed at the end of the chapter, allows students to compare drafts of writing to final versions or writing from the beginning of the year to samples later in the year.

Conclusion

Students who are engaged and self-regulated not only develop lifelong learning habits, they also have higher achievement (Skinner, Wellborn, & Connell, 1990; Tucker et al., 2002). Therefore, teachers like Mr. Calvin in the scenario at the beginning of the chapter can teach history through drama, science through experiments, and read novels aloud to the class and feel confident that they will be improving academic achievement as well as attitudes about learning. The following examples are designed to support student engagement and self-regulation.

Sample Lessons

Simon Says Variation

Purpose: To increase vocabulary learning through movement

Participants: Pre-kindergarten through fifth-grade students

Preparation: The teacher should choose grade-appropriate vocabulary words that have already been introduced and can be shown through facial expressions or movement.

Activity Description

1. Teach students how to play the Simon Says Variation. Students should do what the teacher says to do when he says "Simon Says . . ." If the teacher says to do something but doesn't say "Simon says" first then students should remain still. In the old-fashioned Simon Says, students would be out of the game if they did something that Simon didn't tell them to do, but in the variation, they should do some type of movement and then return to the game. For example, do five jumping jacks in place and re-enter the game. Since this is not an elimination game, it ends when the teacher determines students have played long enough.

2. After doing a couple easy practice rounds, the teacher can begin using the target vocabulary. For young students, Simon might instruct students to put their hands on the "left" side of their desk or "skip" around their desk. Simon might ask older students to show what they would do if they had a "crick" in their neck or how their face would look if they were "anxious."

Modification: After students learn how to play the game, students can take turns being Simon.

Common Core Language Anchor 3: Apply knowledge of language to understand how language functions in different contexts, to make effective choices for meaning or style, and to comprehend more fully when reading or listening.

Biographies

Purpose: For students to read biographies of their choice and at their level. Practice questioning skills.

Participants: Second- through fifth-grade students (see modifications for younger students and developing readers)

Preparation: Find biographies about various people at different reading levels. Encourage students to read biographies that interest them at their independent reading level.

Activity Description

1. Have students choose a biography to read.
2. Students read the biography. Some students may want to read more than one source.
3. The teacher models two different ways students can report on their person. (a) Pretend to be that person and allow other students to ask them questions after a brief introduction of the person. (b) Place a photo of the person on www.blabberize.com and record a message as if you were that person. Save and share with classmates.

Modifications: For younger students or students who lack the independent reading and writing skills necessary for this activity, the teacher can read to the students about a famous person and/or show a movie about a person. Then the teacher can pretend to be that person and allow students to ask questions that would be appropriate for that person. Students should be redirected when they make statements rather than asking questions.

Common Core Writing Anchor 7: Conduct short as well as more sustained research projects based on focused questions, demonstrating understanding of the subject under investigation.

Common Core Speaking and Listening Anchor 1: Prepare for and participate effectively in a range of conversations and collaborations with diverse partners, building on others' ideas and expressing their own clearly and persuasively.

Book Sharing

Purpose: For students to share what they have been reading and develop enthusiasm for reading.

Participants: First- through fifth-grade students

Preparation: Make sure students have access to text at different reading levels and representing a variety of genres. The teacher should find books in advance that she thinks may interest students for the read-aloud portion of the activity.

Activity Description

1. The teacher reads aloud from a book that she thinks may interest the students. For longer books, the teacher may want to read a chapter a day and for shorter books, she should only read the first part of the book. The idea is to get students eager to read the rest of the book on their own. The teacher should explain why she chose that book and what she liked. In addition, the teacher may add comments about wishing the book had more information about particular topics or that a story ended differently.

2. Set up guidelines for students reading silently on their own. For example, how will books be chosen? What happens if a student decides they do not like a book or finishes a book during the quiet reading time? (The teacher may want to place children's magazines around the room for these students. It can be very disruptive if students are constantly getting up and down during quiet reading time.) Will students be allowed to do their reading on the computer or an e-book reader? How long will be devoted to silent reading each day?

3. The teacher walks around the room, quietly asking students about the books that they are reading. She doesn't need to speak to every student every day but should talk with each student at least once a week. Students could be asked to read a favorite part to check whether the reading is at the right level for the student. Questions could be asked about characters, settings, or problems in fictional books. If students are reading nonfiction, they may be asked if they have learned anything new from the book or why they think the author wrote the book. The teacher can also reinforce skills and strategies learned during reading instruction.

4. Students will share what they have read with a partner or small group. Make sure that everyone has an opportunity to share.

5. Once a week, encourage a few students to share what they have been reading with the whole class.

6. Be prepared to set up systems for determining who gets to read popular books next. Teachers report students are anxious to read books that their classmates enjoyed and shared with them.

Common Core Reading Anchor 10: Read and comprehend complex literary and informational texts independently and proficiently.

Common Core Speaking and Listening Anchor 1: Prepare for and participate effectively in a range of conversations and collaborations with diverse partners, building on others' ideas and expressing their own clearly and persuasively.

Portfolio

Purpose: For students to evaluate their own work for both strengths and weaknesses. For students to become self-regulated learners.

Participants: Kindergarten through fifth-grade students

Preparation: The teacher should decide how portfolios will be kept. There are a number of choices including simple file folders, manila envelopes, boxes, and/or computer e-portfolios. The type of portfolio selected will determine what can be placed into it.

Activity Description
1. Provide students with criteria for placing items into the portfolio. What types of items will be placed into the portfolio? Writing samples, worksheets, audio recordings, artwork, presentation materials? Provide students with guidelines for choosing samples to place in the portfolio. For example, students may want to place different drafts of the same writing assignment in the portfolio so they can review how their writing progressed from the first draft to the final product.
2. Have students explain why they chose a particular item to place in the portfolio. This can be done orally with very young children, with a check sheet with early readers and writers, and with short essays for more advanced students.

3. Have students describe orally or in writing at least two things that they are proud of in their work. Then have them choose one area for improvement and discuss how they might go about meeting that goal. Teachers should help students set relatively narrow, obtainable goals. For example, improving math skills is too broad but getting better at double digit subtraction problems is a workable objective.

Common Core Writing Anchor 10 (one example of how portfolios correlate with Common Core): Write routinely over extended time frames (time for research, reflection, and revision) and shorter time frames (a single sitting or a day or two) for a range of tasks, purposes, and audiences.

References

Gallimore, R., & Tharp, R. G. (1990). Teaching mind in society. In L.C. Moll (Ed.), *Vygotsky and education: Instructional implications and applications of sociohistorical psychology* (p. 175–205). Cambridge, England: Cambridge University Press.

Harris, B. (2013, March 26). 7 easy-to-use-conversational strategies for the Common Core. [Webinar]. Retrieved from www.eyeoneducation.com

Hattie, J. (2012). *Visible learning for teachers: Maximizing impact on learning.* New York, NY: Routledge.

Jensen, E. (2000). Moving with the brain in mind. *Educational Leadership, 58*(3), 34–37.

Lavy, V. (2007). Using performance-based pay to improve the quality of teachers. *Future of Children, 17*(1), 87–109. Retrieved from http://futureofchildren.org/futureofchildren/publications/docs/17_01_05.pdf

Lee, S., Nihiser, A., Fulton, J., Borgogna, B., & Zavacky, F. (2012). Physical education and physical activity: Results from the school health policies and practices study 2012. In *Results from the School Health Policies and Practices Study 2012,* US Department of Health and Human Services Centers for Disease Control and Prevention.

Nicholson, E. (2013, April 2). Arlington High suspends student for tweeting STAAR test photo, inspires predictable backlash. *Dallas

Observer online. Retrieved from http://blogs.dallasobserver.com/unfairpark/2013/04/arlington_high_suspends_stud en.php

Ohanian, S. (2002). *What happened to recess and why are our children struggling in kindergarten.* New York, NY: McGraw Hill.

Perkins-Gough, D., & Duckworth, A. L. (2013). The Significance of GRIT. *Educational Leadership, 71*(1), 14–20.

Pianta, R. C., Belsky, J., Houts, R., & Morrison, F. (2007). Opportunities to learn in America's elementary classrooms. *Science, 315*(30), 1795–1796.

Pink, D. H. (2011). *Drive: The surprising truth about what motivates us.* New York, NY: Riverhead.

Skinner, E. A., Wellborn, J. G., & Connell, J. P. (1990). What it takes to do well in school and whether I've got it: A process model of perceived control and children's engagement and achievement in school. *Journal of Educational Psychology, 82*(1), 22–32. doi:10.1037/0022–0663.82.1.22

Tucker, C. M., Zayco, R. A., Herman, K. C., Reinke, W. M., Trujillo, M., Carraway, K., Wallack, C., & Ivery, P. D. (2002). Teacher and child variables as predictors of academic engagement among low-income African American children. *Psychology in the Schools, 39*(4), 477–488.

Wagner, T. (2008). *The global achievement gap: Why even our best schools don't teach the new survival skills our children need—and what to do about it.* New York, NY: Basic Books.

Other Resources

Morrow, L. M., Tracey, D. H., Woo, D. G., & Pressley, M. (1999). Characteristics of exemplary first-grade literacy instruction. *The Reading Teacher, 52*(5), 462–476.

Recording information for playback with moving mouths: www.blabberize.com

Collaborators

Positive interdependence does more than simply motivate individuals to try harder; it facilitates the development of new insights and discoveries and the more frequent use of higher level reasoning strategies.

Johnson & Johnson, 2009, p. 368

Scenario
Cooperative Learning

Ms. Rossi was in her second year of teaching second grade. Overall, she was pleased with her teaching and her students' progress. Her mentor teacher, Mr. Harris, had been extremely helpful, especially when she sought help with classroom management during the first year. The principal had made sure they had opportunities to observe each other teaching and discuss their observations. One thing she had observed and liked about Mr. Harris's classroom was student cooperative learning. The students seemed much more engaged in their learning than during whole class or independent work. It also gave Mr. Harris time to conference with individual students or small groups that needed extra assistance. Although Ms. Rossi wanted to try it, she was afraid it would create classroom management challenges. She also didn't know how she would cover all the required material with student cooperative learning. Ms. Rossi decided to ask Mr. Harris for help with cooperative learning.

Mr. Harris was more than happy to assist Ms. Rossi's efforts in implementing cooperative learning. He was appreciative of the extra time his school leader made available for mentors and novice teachers to meet. More cooperative learning and less whole group instruction would enhance student learning by providing the needed time to work individually with students.

Cooperative Learning and Classroom Management

Ms. Rossi is not alone in being afraid that cooperative learning will increase classroom management issues. It is true that the classroom will be noisier during cooperative learning than during individual work time, but other management problems can be minimized with careful implementation. True cooperative learning goes beyond simply putting students into groups. In cooperative learning, students have clearly defined team goals and each student understands his or her individual and group responsibilities.

When starting cooperative learning with a class, teachers should begin small—by that we mean that students should be paired rather than placed in groups of three or more. The time given for the cooperative learning and the purpose should be clear. The following are a few examples of how cooperative learning can be integrated into instruction without creating classroom management challenges. More ideas are provided at the end of the chapter.

Turn and Talk

One good way to begin cooperative learning with a new class is Turn and Talk. Each student sits next to a partner and the teacher will occasionally stop an activity and ask students to turn and talk. For example, the teacher might be getting ready to read a book about transportation. He can give the partners 30 seconds to think of different types of transportation. The teacher should have a clear way of indicating the 30 seconds are up and that students need to pay attention again. Then the teacher should say something like "let's read to see if the book has the same ideas that you and your partner had" and continue reading. The purpose of this type of activity is to get everyone thinking about the topic of the book without having them raise their hand and make comments one by one. Turn and Talk can be used during almost any type of teacher-led activity throughout the day.

For Turn and Talk and other partner activities, careful consideration should be given to who is partnered together. Begin making the list with students who need the most support from partners. If a child is a beginning English language learner, try to partner that child with someone who speaks his native language but has more advanced English skills. Place students who are patient with students who struggle. Partnering the most advanced student with the one who needs the most support is probably not a good idea because both students are likely to get frustrated, and the more advanced students may dominate the discussions. On the other hand, partnering the student with the most social skills with one who is weaker in that area is a good idea, as the student with strong social skills will be able to make up for the weakness of the other student. Some students may partner for Turn and Talk, but have different partners for math, reading, or writing. "Thinking about what kind of support you want the partners to provide for the various activities and assigning partners purposefully is the secret to the success of this collaborative grouping" (Cunningham & Allington, 2011, p. 221).

Shared Reading

Another way that teachers often use partners is for paired reading. First the teacher needs to determine how he wants the students to read, for example, take turns every other page. Then decide what students will do when one of them makes a mistake but keeps reading and what to do if one of the students gets stuck. Choose an outgoing student and model the way students should read with the teacher reading and making mistakes and the student responding in the manner that you have instructed them.

Teachers need to be sure that students have a purpose for reading, which could be answering questions posed during pre-reading activities, jotting down new vocabulary words, or marking three interesting points with sticky notes. They also should have a strict time limit, even if that means a few students don't finish. "Most behavior problems during partner reading happen when children have time to fool around" (Cunningham & Allington, 2011, p. 223). When pairs complete their reading assignment early, it is important that students know what they should do. For example, they can come up with two questions about the text they just read and trade with another pair that is finished. These "extra" assignments or fillers may not be completed but never-the-less encourage more thinking about the reading.

If students need to read a particular text, such as a social studies book that may be difficult for some students, partner them with a strong reader. The strong reader does all the reading but the other reader asks questions based on each heading in the book before the reading and tries to answer them when that section is read. Of course, all students need to read independent and instructional level material some time during the day, but there are times when the teacher needs to use more advanced materials because other materials on the topic are not readily available.

Partner activities can be used in similar ways for problem solving in math or peer-editing in writing. Just as with partner reading, there should be a clear purpose for the activity, procedures for the activity should be demonstrated by the teacher, students should know how much time they have, and they should have thoughtful activities to do when they complete the assignment.

Working with Larger Groups

Working in groups of three or four presents greater challenges than working in pairs. Activities should be structured to make sure that each student in the group participates and that there is a group goal that encourages students to work together toward a common objective. One of the problems that often occurs when students are working in groups is that some students dominate and others do not participate. The smaller the group, the easier it is to avoid this problem. There are a number of ways to make sure each individual actively participates in the group activity.

One of them is to give each student in the group a specific role. This may differ with the particular activity, grade level, and subject matter but some student roles are discussion director, vocabulary enricher, recorder, illustrator, researcher, materials manager, and reporter. Since groups in elementary school should be no larger than four, no more than four of these roles will be used for any particular activity.

Another way to make sure everyone in a group has an opportunity to talk is to give each person in the group three tokens with their own color. Each time someone in the group talks, they give up a token. If a person runs out of tokens, they cannot speak again until everyone has used up their tokens, and the process is started again.

The Different Colored Markers activity at the end of the chapter is another way to make sure everyone participates. No matter what type of cooperative learning strategy is used, it is important that teachers make their expectations clear, give the groups a purpose for working together, monitor the students' progress, provide time limits, and have filler activities for those who finish early. Activities should be designed so that everyone is actively engaged and learning from one another.

Covering All the Material

The second major concern that teachers have about cooperative learning is that it takes too much time. Helping students succeed in cooperative learning does take time. Certainly, it would be much quicker for the teacher to get up in front of the room and cover the material, but study after study has shown that students learn better in almost every subject area when they work cooperatively in pairs or small groups than in classrooms where instruction is dominated by teacher instruction followed by individual practice (Gillies, 2002; Yager, Johnson, Johnson, & Snider, 1986). When collaboration is implemented properly, students learn social skills as well as content. This can result in higher self-esteem, more friends, and improved attitudes toward school (Schul, 2011).

Teachers concerned about the slower pace of cooperative learning can apply *less is more* ideas. They can ask themselves if there is anything that can be cut from the curriculum or combined. Can students read fewer selections from the reading, social studies, or science books? Can students do fewer practice problems or reading worksheets? Are some things taught a certain way simply because it has always been done that way? Can topics be combined through integrated units? (Chapter 2 offers more details about cutting and combining to save time.) The class may cover less material, but students will learn it better.

Teachers may also ask themselves if they can split the work among the students. For example, one student in a pair can work four problems and the partner work on four other problems. Then they can switch papers and check the other one's work, asking questions along the way. If they disagree on the problem-solving process or answer, they can work together to figure it out. This type of assignment has the advantages of both individual and pair work. Each student only works four problems, but they are held responsible for all eight.

Integrated units also can be divided up with students becoming "experts" in different parts of the unit rather than everyone reading all the material. One way to do this is to come up with six or seven different aspects within a topic. Students then choose a first, second, and third choice. They are divided up so there are no more than four in each group. For example, a study of a state might be divided into people, geography, arts and culture, agriculture, industries, plants and animals, and major cities. Each group would study their topic and present their information to the whole class through a poster, PowerPoint, or other means. By dividing up the material, the class can cover more material and still reap the advantages of collaboration. This idea is discussed further in the Divide and Conquer activity at the end of the chapter.

Other Challenges to Collaborative Work

The communication skills of students is another challenge to collaborative work. We have all had the experience of coming away from a conversation thinking, "I wonder what she meant by that." We also may have had experiences when we have misinterpreted what someone else said. Collaboration requires communication and effective communication occurs when we can explain ourselves effectively and correctly interpret what others are communicating. This is one of the reasons that Common Core recommends teaching listening and speaking skills through collaborative work.

Young children begin to learn collaboration skills through play. The more opportunities children have to play with each other, the more likely they will learn to better pick up each others' signals. So opportunities for play like recess or even classroom play help children develop the social skills needed to become effective collaborators. This is true in both early childhood as children learn to pretend together, all the way up through upper elementary where children organize games and activities that require shared rules for participating. Learning that certain rules must be followed in order to keep the activity going is an important skill for children. In many cases these skills develop naturally, and teacher interference in settling disputes may actually impede the development of these important social skills. On the other hand, when bullying is occurring there should be adult intervention. Also, when one child is being intentionally excluded from a group, adults may be needed to see why that child is being excluded.

Unfortunately, some children have more trouble than others developing social skills. Role-play may help students understand how to deal with some of the natural conflicts that arise during collaborative work. Just as with other types of play, children participating in role-play know that they are just pretending. The teacher can play the role of the difficult student and give other students an opportunity to role play with her in front of the class. Puppets are also an effective way of introducing social skills with children. Having the puppet say or do something rude or inappropriate allows the demonstration of the behavior without a person having to engage in the behavior. The children can then comment on what the puppet did without having to say something to a person.

Conclusion

Collaborative learning offers many advantages for students and teachers despite some of the challenges. Direct instruction is still important when introducing new concepts, but collaborative work allows students to develop deeper understanding of ideas, communication strategies, and social skills. The following examples demonstrate ways to incorporate cooperative learning into elementary school instruction.

Sample Lessons

Different Colored Markers

Participants: Kindergarten through fifth-grade students

Purpose: To encourage communication, higher-order thinking, and group participation.

Preparation: Decide how many students will be in each group. Obtain enough different colored markers, crayons, or colored pencils so that each student in a group has a different colored writing utensil. Provide each group with one piece of paper or overhead transparency if answers will be shared on the overhead.

Activity Description
1. Ask students an open-ended question related to the current theme. For example, younger students might be asked to name a type of fruit or vegetable and be allowed to draw it. Students in the middle grades could list character traits of a character in a book the whole class read or listened to. Older students might be asked to write an opinion statement and give reasons to support the opinion.
2. After the assignment has been given, students take turns drawing or writing on the same sheet of paper. Students must write only with their own color. As the teacher walks around the room, he can easily see if all the students are participating by checking to see if all the colors have been used.

Extension: The group activity could be used as a springboard for more in-depth activities. The younger students could write and illustrate books about healthy foods. The students who wrote about character traits could write a more in-depth description of the character and what would happen if the character came to their classroom, and the students who wrote reasons to support their opinions could research the reasons and write a short paper or do a PowerPoint supporting their opinion.

Divide and Conquer

Participants: Third- through fifth-grade students

Purpose: To divide reading and encourage group participation.

Preparation: Choose a nonfiction chapter the class is going to read, such as from the science or social studies book. Divide the chapter up into five to eight parts by subheadings if possible. Then divide the class up into the same number of groups as there are parts in the chapter. There should be no more than four in a group.

Activity Description
1. Introduce the topic of the chapter and make sure that students understand vocabulary crucial to understanding the chapter.
2. Assign roles to each student in the group. It is helpful to hand out cards with an explanation of the assigned roles to the students who will be doing those jobs. Some appropriate roles for this assignment would be discussion leader, recorder, summarizer, and presenter.
3. Have students read only the part of the chapter assigned to their group. They can read silently if everyone can read the chapter independently or one of the better readers in the group can read it aloud if some of the group members may struggle with the reading.
4. The discussion leader helps the group discuss the main points of their section while the recorder writes down those points.

5. The discussion leader gets chart paper, an overhead transparency, a computer, or some other media that can be shown to the whole class.
6. The group summarizes the main points of their section and the summarizer writes them down in a form they can present to the class.
7. When all groups have completed steps three through six, they will present to the class.

Notes: This activity will usually require at least two days.

The same type of activity can be done in which each group reads a different text about the same topic, followed by the presentation.

References

Cunningham, P. M., & Allington, R. L. (2011). *Classrooms that work: They can all read and write* (5th ed.). Boston, MA: Pearson.

Gillies, R. M. (2002). The residual effects of cooperative-learning experiences: A two-year follow-up. *Journal of Educational Research, 96*(1), 15–20. doi:10.1080/00220670209598787

Johnson, D. W., & Johnson, R. T. (2009). An educational psychology success story: Social interdependence theory and cooperative learning. *Educational Researcher, 38*(5), 365–379.

Schul, J. E. (2011). Revisiting an old friend: The practice and promise of cooperative learning for the twenty-first century. *Social Studies, 102*(2), 88. doi:10.1080/00377996.2010.509370

Yager, S., Johnson, R. T., Johnson, D. W., & Snider, B. (1986). The impact of group processing on achievement in cooperative learning groups. *Journal of Social Psychology, 126*(3), 389–397. doi:10.1080/00224545.1986.9713601

Other Resources

Aronson, E. (2008). *Jigsaw classroom.* Retrieved from www.jigsaw.org

Kagan, S. (1999, Winter). Cooperative learning: Seventeen pros and seventeen cons plus ten tips for success. *Kagan Online Magazine.* Retrieved from www.kaganonline.com/free_articles/dr_spencer_kagan/ASK06.php

Slavin, R. E. (1991). Synthesis of research on cooperative learning. *Educational Leadership, 48*(5), 71–82.

8

Getting the Most Out
of Assessment

I didn't fail the test, I just found 100 ways to do it wrong.

Benjamin Franklin

Scenario
Data for What?

Ms. Scott was considered one of the best, most organized teachers at the school. When it came to standardized tests, she was even more organized. She had benchmarks prepared for the 20 weeks of school before the date of the state exam. Every Friday was benchmark day. When she had graded the exams each child's score was entered into an Excel file. She knew which children scored low and which ones high. She knew if the scores went up and when they went down. She pretty much knew what each child would score on the state exam based on all her data. She was regularly asked to make presentations to the school faculty about her data collection process.

At the faculty meeting just before benchmarking began, Ms. Scott was again asked to describe her complex and detailed data collection process. Toward the end of the presentation one of the first-year teachers raised her hand and asked, "So just what do we use all this data for?" Ms. Scott and the principal just stared for a moment.

"Do we use it to change instruction in some way?"

That one question started a year-long debate at the school about how they were assessing the children's progress and what they were using the information for. At the end of the school year, Ms. Scott shredded all her benchmark exams and started using some of the processes described in this chapter.

Integrating Assessment into Instruction

When assessment is integrated into instruction, it interrupts instruction less and provides more useful information for learning, reflecting *less is more*. All kinds of assessments, including tests, can be used as formative assessment during learning. Unlike the benchmarks mentioned in the scenario at the beginning of the chapter, formative assessment is used to provide feedback to students and to adjust instruction during the lesson or soon thereafter.

Darling-Hammond (2014) says, "A 21st century education system has no place for the antiquated distinction between teaching and testing. Modern assessments should provide valuable information to educators on their practice as well as insights about how individual students are doing" (p. 12).

Douglas County School District in Colorado is an example of a district that is placing more emphasis on formative assessments so they can gain more information about each student's learning throughout the year. "Douglas County started developing its own performance assessments in 2011 to try and measure the kind of thinking and doing students would need for the real world" (Schwartz, 2014, para. 6).

Teachers do formative assessments every day even if they don't call it that. Teachers are conducting formative assessment when they listen to students' answers to questions, observe students conducting a science experiment, or listen to partners solve a problem. To make it a little more formal, teachers can make a few anecdotal notes on labels about these observations and then place them into a student's folder after school. Even if the teacher only makes notes about five or six students a day, most elementary school teachers will have notes about the whole class by the end of the week. Here are a few more ways teachers can incorporate assessment into instruction regularly.

Quick Assessments

If teachers want to get a quick assessment of students' understanding of a topic that they are currently discussing, they can provide each student with a small dry erase board, a marker, and something that will erase the board. After introducing a new topic, ask a few short-answer questions and have students write the answer on their boards. This can even be used to check procedural knowledge, such as what they will do first when they begin writing that day. A similar quick check can be provided by having students complete a one or two question quiz on an index card.

Student Self-Assessment

Students also can self-assess their understanding of a topic. For example, as students complete math problems, they can be asked to rank each problem with a "U" for understand this type of problem and "NS" for not sure or as confident about doing these types of problems. Most students will accurately assess their own knowledge and skills if there is no penalty for doing so. This will help the teacher quickly see which types of problems have been mastered by most of the students and which require more work. Students also can use rubrics prepared by the teacher to evaluate and modify their own work before handing it in. Writing and Using Rubrics at the end of the chapter provides more information about the use of rubrics by students and teachers.

Running Records

While students are reading, a teacher can take students aside individually to conduct a running record in which he listens to students read a short passage and records their errors or miscues. The type of errors and corrections made help teachers understand more about the students' strengths and needs. For example, if a student reads "home" instead of "house," they understand the meaning of the sentence, but if they read "horse" instead of "house," they may be depending too heavily on phonetic cues. This information can be used for further instruction and shared with students to help them adjust their own reading strategies.

Multiple Assessments at Once

Some assignments may provide information about several things at once. After reading about the Underground Railroad, the teacher might ask students to summarize what they have learned. These summaries will help the teacher learn whether students understand the Underground Railroad, know how to summarize information, and know how to organize their ideas in writing. Assignments such as these can easily be integrated into instruction and provide valuable information for student feedback and improving instruction.

Analyzing the Results

When choosing assessments and analyzing the results, it is important to know what the results really mean. A story from my son's third-grade class illustrates this point. When I went in for a conference with the teacher, I was told that he was having trouble comprehending what he read. I really couldn't understand this because he always seemed to be able to discuss what he read at home. It was only at the end of the year, when he received high scores on the state reading exam that I realized what had happened. During the year, the teacher had him read aloud to her from new material and then asked comprehension questions. He had a lisp and was so concerned about how he was pronouncing the words that his comprehension suffered. When he read silently and then answered comprehension questions, he was much more successful. This exemplifies why it is important to use a variety of different assessments throughout the year and to analyze what the results mean for each student. Additional ideas are provided in Variety of Formative Assessments at the end of the chapter.

Using a Variety of Assessments

Each type of assessment, whether it is a rubric for a writing assignment or a multiple-choice test for math, has strengths and weaknesses. Each only gives teachers a small picture of students' learning abilities and needs. Therefore, it is essential to use a variety of different types of assessments to truly understand the students in a class.

> Different approaches and formats can yield different diagnostic information to teachers. For example, well-developed multiple choice items contain alternatives that represent common student misconceptions or errors. Short answer item responses can give the teacher information about student's thinking underlying the answer.
> (Miyasaka, 2000, p. 7)

Questions to help teachers select appropriate assessments for their needs are provided in Choosing Formative Assessments at the end of the chapter.

Student Feedback from Assessment

In order for formative assessment to have the greatest impact on achievement and test scores, it must be accompanied by timely and clear feedback for students (Hattie, 2012a). Despite overwhelming research evidence that effective feedback can significantly improve student performance, not all feedback is effective.

One reason that much of the feedback is not effective is that it comes days after the work has been completed, often in the form of graded papers, and after the class has moved on to another assignment rather than during the learning process when students have an opportunity to improve. Think of someone coaching a basketball team. The games against other teams are like tests at the end of a unit, but most of the assessment and feedback goes on before and between games. Players practice various skills, such as dribbling while the coach observes, provides feedback, and asks players to try again, implementing the new suggestions. The coach may ask the players themselves what they think they could do better. Just as the basketball coach provides immediate feedback to players during practice sessions, teachers can give timely feedback to students so they quickly know how they are progressing and what they should do next. "If you give them feedback at the end of the process and then move on, they never have the opportunity to apply what you have shared and improve their performance" (Jackson, 2009, p. 141).

Feedback is most effective when it is individual because students must understand how the feedback applies to their own work. If a teacher simply tells the class that they need to pay more attention to punctuation in their next essays, the students may not know if the comment applies to them, what type of punctuation the teacher wants, or where to learn more about the troublesome punctuation. Teachers also should avoid making comments about what individual students need to do in front of their peers, thus embarrassing the student and creating a poor atmosphere for risk-taking and learning from errors. Comments should be made individually either in writing or orally. This is why it is important for students to work either independently or in small groups while the teacher conferences with individual students.

In addition to being timely and individual, feedback based on assessment needs to provide students with a clear direction about what they should do next. "If this *Where to next part* is missing, students are likely to ignore, misinterpret, or fail to act on the feedback they hear. They need to know where to put their effort and attention" (Hattie, 2012b, p. 20). For instance, if a student simply receives an 80 percent on a math assignment, it doesn't help her know what she could do to correct her work or improve next time. Instead, the teacher might grade the math assignment in which the student showed how she solved the problems. If the student had incorrect answers, she should have an opportunity to rework the problems and find out where in the process the mistake was made. As students are working on these corrections, the teacher can spot check and ask students what caused their mistakes and discuss with them how it could be prevented the next time they have similar problems. The assignment will then be regraded and the student will receive the new grade. This demonstrates to students that they are doing the work to learn rather than just to earn a grade. Since allowing students to redo assignments requires more time, teachers should give fewer and shorter graded assignments as per *less is more*. Students who succeed the first time should be given enrichment or challenge activities rather than being required to do more of the same type of work.

Using Information from Assessments to Modify Instruction

Hoping to lose weight and weighing myself daily without making changes in my diet or exercise regime is similar to teachers who assess their students but do not use the results to modify their instruction. We are not likely to see any positive changes.

Assessments, in addition to providing information about individual student's progress, can also be useful in providing information about the skills and knowledge of the whole class. Pre-assessments, such as quizzes or brainstorming activities, can provide information about students' knowledge and attitudes concerning a topic they are about to study. It was through one of these activities that I learned some of my students thought dinosaurs still lived in Africa.

Assessments conducted during a unit can help the teacher determine what steps to take next. If only a few students are struggling with a skill, the teacher can conduct small group sessions to support those students, but if a majority of students need support with a skill, then the teacher should review and reteach, perhaps using a different approach. When assessments reveal major holes in understanding, Calkins, Ehrenworth, and Lehman (2012) recommend not starting with the most challenging work. "Often, backing up a bit to get a good start helps all learners have enough steam to overcome the tougher bits" (p. 178).

Preparing for Common Core and Other High-Stakes Assessments

By now some educators are probably saying to themselves, "Formative assessment is well and good, but I have to prepare my students for high-stakes testing at the end of the year." Aligning teaching to the standards, conducting regular formative assessment, providing high-quality feedback to students, and adjusting instruction based on formative assessment will go a long way toward preparing for high-stakes assessments, but they are not enough.

Time should be spent throughout the year familiarizing students with both the vocabulary and format of the assessments they will take at the end of the year. If possible this should be done with some assessments for the integrated units that mimic the format and vocabulary of the test. This will allow teachers and students to continue to focus on the topic at hand rather than using test-preparation materials that have students focus on completely different subjects and often can't be used for student feedback or instructional modifications. For example, if the tests use a multiple choice format, students should become familiar with these formats as well as ways to eliminate incorrect answers if they are not sure of the correct one. Many tests ask students the meaning of a word in a specific sentence or paragraph of a text. Students need practice returning to the text to find out how the word is used in context.

The vocabulary of standardized tests also may be different than is normally used in class. For example, students may be asked to choose the statement that provides *evidence* of one of the author's messages so teachers need to make an effort to use the term in this way during class instruction. If students are asked to write an *equation* showing how they would solve a problem, they need to understand what is meant by an *equation* in this context.

As this book is being written, the Common Core assessments are still being constructed and field-tested, and many questions remain. They are being written by two organizations, the Partnership for Assessment of Readiness for College and Careers (PARCC) and the Smarter Balanced Assessment Consortium. Both organizations have promised that the assessments will closely reflect most of the Common Core standards.

Computer-Administered Assessments

Although the assessments for the Common Core have not been completed, both state consortiums plan to administer the test via computer. Other states are also moving toward computer-administered exams. Not only do schools need to have the appropriate computers available and back-up plans for technology glitches, they also need to make sure that students have appropriate amounts of time to practice using the computer for test-taking. Some of the test-taking skills that have previously been taught, such as marking reading passages on a printed exam may not be possible. Other things, such as revising and editing writing, may become easier with these new computer-administered exams. Computer-administered exams also may require new skills for some students. For example, sample questions on the PARCC site required dragging and dropping multiple sentences into boxes.

Therefore, time should be spent familiarizing students with the format and vocabulary of the high-stakes assessments. They also will need to become confident of appropriate computer skills so the use of the computer for the exam doesn't negatively impact their scores. As much as possible, this should be integrated into the regular curriculum rather than becoming a daily dose of drill and practice. (Additional information about computer-administered assessments is provided in Chapter 12.)

Using the Results from High-Stakes Assessments

Almost all research on assessment supports using a variety of assessments to make educational decisions about students, teachers, schools, and programs (Darling-Hammond, 2014), yet many states and districts primarily base important decisions, such as grade retention, on one end of the year test. Teachers, administrators, and others concerned about education should encourage the use of multiple sources of data to make important decisions. At the very least, teachers should use a combination of information when trying to learn about students at the beginning of the year.

Even well-designed tests have limitations. Time limits how many items can be tested so the questions only represent a sample of the standards. Tests also tend to depend heavily on multiple-choice questions because they are faster to take and to grade, making them less expensive for districts and ultimately taxpayers.

For the next few years, special care should be taken in using the results of assessments based on the Common Core. The Common Core standards, which are like steps going up from kindergarten through fifth grade, differ significantly from many previous state standards. Therefore, if a school implemented instruction based on the Common Core standards during the 2012–2013 school year, it will be 2017–2018 before a fifth grader will have received the full benefit of instruction based on the Common Core standards from kindergarten through fifth grade.

Conclusion

In conclusion, most decisions about standardized testing are made at the state level so local educators and school boards have little control over these policies, but they can control how students are prepared for the tests. Educators can prepare students for testing without so many of the negative side effects. There should be less emphasis on test preparation materials and benchmark tests and more on formative assessments that provide valuable information to both students and teachers. Students can be ready for standardized testing and still learn social studies, science, communication skills, collaboration, decision making, and many of the other topics that are often left out of elementary school education. Teachers can differentiate instruction so that all students are progressing throughout the school year. The following activities are designed to help educators choose and use assessment in more productive ways.

Assessment Examples

Choosing Formative Assessments

Purpose: To help educators and others choose formative assessments that will provide them with needed information for student feedback and improvement of instruction.

Participants: Educators or others who are choosing formative assessments to use with elementary school students

Questions: The following are questions and notations that may help educators and others select assessments that will best fit their needs.

1. What is the purpose of the assessment?
Different types of assessments are better for different purposes. For example, a standardized reading test provides information that allows educational leaders to assess the impact of a new reading program when the same assessment is used before and after implementation. However, standardized reading tests are not the best vehicle for gaining information to provide individual student feedback. A student who does poorly on the standardized test might have trouble with decoding words, English vocabulary, comprehension strategies, or other reading skills, but these are best identified with an informal reading inventory rather than standardized tests.

2. Have the students been taught all the skills needed to be successful on the assessment?
Although educators sometimes use assessments that include items that students have not yet learned in class to determine what they still need to learn, these types of assessments are very frustrating for students who want to do well on the assessment. They may also develop bad attitudes

about assessments, and students may not even try on important end of the year high-stakes exams.

3.   How much will the assessments interrupt instruction?
When schools have frequent benchmark exams to prepare for the end of the year tests, as discussed in the scenario at the beginning of the chapter, a great deal of time is taken away from real reading, writing, and problem solving. Although some practice tests are certainly necessary, much assessment can be done as part of instruction, such as using a rubric to assess student presentations.

4.   What information will the assessment provide for student feedback?
Assessment best helps improve student achievement when it provides information that students can use to improve their work, such as individual teacher-student conferences during writing time.

5.   What information will the assessment provide to modify instruction?
Assessments that are conducted during instruction, such as during an integrated unit, will give teachers immediate feedback on what students understand and what work they still need to do. This helps teachers adjust their instruction before moving on to the next topic or concept.

6.   Is the assessment analyzing something in addition to the targeted skill?
The most common example of this in elementary school is assessments with math word problems. Some students may have trouble with the reading and others with the math problem-solving process. In this case, the teacher can try reading the problems to students to determine whether students are struggling with the reading or math problem-solving process or both.

7.   Will this assessment add variety to the type of assessments already being used?
Each type of assessment has strengths and weaknesses. Therefore, it is important to use a wide range of assessments during the school year to pinpoint student strengths and needs.

8.   Does the assessment help prepare students for high-stakes testing? Although high-stakes test preparation should not dominate the curriculum or assessment, students do need to learn the vocabulary and format of the standardized tests. They also need to gain the computer skills needed to be successful on computer-administered tests.

Writing and Using Rubrics

Purpose: To provide rubrics that can be used by teachers to assess students' work and provide specific feedback to students. To provide rubrics that students can use to understand the teachers' expectations and self-assess their own work.

Participants: First- through fifth-grade teachers and students

Description
1.   Choose what the rubric will be used for. It is best to use the same rubric throughout the year for the same type of work so that students understand the expectations for that type of work and teachers don't have to keep creating new rubrics. Some ways that rubrics might be used are for assessing presentations, projects, or different types of writing.
2.   Decide what criteria will be included in the rubric. For example, a rubric for presentations might include criteria for content accuracy, focus on topic, use of visuals, oral presentation, and ability to answer questions from peers.
3.   Decide what an effective performance on each of the criteria would look like. Then decide what a less than effective performance would be. Rubrics usually have between three and five performance levels (see Table 8.1).
4.   Decide how much of the grade each part of the rubric is worth. For example, content of an informational paper may be worth more than mechanics on the same paper. This can be indicated by a multiplier, such as x10 for content, which would mean a full score on content would be 5 x 10 or 50.

TABLE 8.1 Part of a Five Performance-Level Rubric for an Argumentative Paper

1	2	3	4	5
No reason supporting argument and/or no supporting evidence.	One reason supporting argument and/or almost no evidence supporting reasoning.	Two reasons supporting argument or three reasons with little clear evidence for the reasons.	Three reasons supporting argument. Evidence provided for some of the reasons is not clear.	Three reasons supporting argument. Each reason is clearly supported by evidence.

5. Present and explain the rubric to students before they are asked to do the assignment. If possible, give students examples that have been assessed using the rubric so they can see what the scores actually look like for a completed project or paper. Students may also be given opportunities to assess other projects or papers with the rubric to see how close their analysis is to the teacher's.

6. Encourage students to assess their own work using the rubric before handing it in or presenting it to the class.

Note: Grade-level teachers may want to work together to develop rubrics. This saves each teacher time and allows teachers, if desired, to switch papers with another teacher and assess them using the common rubric to provide a more objective assessment.

Younger students may not be able to apply rubrics themselves.

Variety of Formative Assessments

Purpose: To provide educators ways to incorporate more formative assessments in their classrooms for student feedback and instructional improvement. These are in addition to those already mentioned in the chapter.

Participants: Pre-K–5th teachers

Portfolios—Student work samples are included in these portfolios, which can be done in many ways, including boxes, folders, or online. Portfolios are most often used for writing samples, but also can be used for problem-solving samples, recordings, research projects, and other work. They allow teachers, students, and families to view the type of work the student is doing and the progression throughout the year.

Checklists—Checklists provide a quick way for teachers to record student progress. For example, the teacher might have a checklist for math that includes such items as "able to add two digit numbers together" or "able to identify the correct strategy(ies) to solve a problem." The checklists could include the date the item was checked and a "+, ?, or –" for each item. Checklists also can be used for things such as collaboration skills, ability to work independently, or perseverance on a project.

Performance Tasks—Students demonstrate their skills by actually doing something, such as a science investigation, skit, research presentation, or art project. These can be assessed in different ways, such as using a rubric, a checklist, or notes that are placed in a notebook or student folder.

Quick Write—Give students two to five minutes to write on an index card or slip of paper. They may be asked to summarize what they read, explain important vocabulary in their own words, or list the steps in the scientific process.

Graphic Organizers—Graphic organizers can be used for almost any subject but all provide students with a structure for providing information. Some examples are: Venn diagrams that help students compare and contrast two or three things, story maps that help students identify the main parts of a story, main idea and detail outlines, and problem-solving graphic organizers that ask students to fill in specific steps they use as they solve a problem.

Peer Feedback—Before a presentation is made to the class or an assignment is handed in to the teacher, students provide each other with constructive feedback. Teachers need to model how this feedback should be given and provide criteria or rubrics to help improve the usefulness of peer feedback.

Drawing—Visual representations through drawing or from the computer can serve as formative assessments for many topics. For example, students can be asked to show a math problem through a drawing or illustrate a vocabulary word. This may be particularly useful for students who have difficulty with writing but enjoy drawing.

Sticky Notes—Students place sticky notes in texts to mark items rather than copying them down. For example, the teacher might ask students to mark three details that support the author's main idea while they are reading. The teacher can monitor where students are placing these notes. Or these notes can be used as the basis for a class discussion after reading.

Beach Ball—The teacher plays music and the students pass the beach ball around the classroom. The student with the ball when the music stops, must answer a question. This is a good way to review material or determine whether students understood text or presentations. Care must be taken not to embarrass students in front of their peers.

References

Calkins, L., Ehrenworth, M., & Lehman, C. (2012). *Pathways to the Common Core: Accelerating achievement.* Portsmouth, NH: Heinemann.

Darling-Hammond, L. (2014). Testing to, and beyond the Common Core. *Principal, 93*(3), 8–12.

Hattie, J. (2012a). Know thy IMPACT. *Educational Leadership, 70*(1), 18–23.

Hattie, J. (2012b). *Visible learning for teachers: Maximizing impact on learning.* New York, NY: Routledge.

Jackson, R. R. (2009). *Never work harder than your students and other principles of great teaching.* Alexandria, VA: ASCD.

Miyasaka, J. R. (2000). A framework for evaluating the validity of test preparation practices. Retrieved from ERIC database. (ED454256)

Schwartz, K. (2014, April 2). *Can schools be held accountable without standardized tests?* Retrieved from http://blogs.kqed.org/mindshift/2014/04/can-schools-be- held-accountable-without-standardized-tests/

Other Resources

Au, W. (2007). High-stakes testing and curricular control: A qualitative metasynthesis. *Educational Researcher, 36*(5), 258–267.

Formative assessment. http://assessment.tki.org.nz/

Levinson, M. (2014, March 14). Re: The importance of play in preparing for standardized testing. Retrieved from www.edutopia.org/blog/play-with-standardized-test-prep-matt-levinson

Marzano, R.J. (2010). *Formative assessment & standards-based grading.* Bloomington, IN: Marzano Research Laboratory.

Marzano, R.J., Yanoski, D. C., Hoegh, J.K., Simms, J.A. with Heflebower, T. & Warrick, P. (2013). *Using Common Core standards to enhance classroom instruction & assessment.* Bloomington, IN: Marzano Research Laboratory.

Partnership for Assessment of Readiness for College and Careers (PARCC) Common Core Assessment. www.parcconline.org

Ravitch, D. (2010). *The death and life of the great American school system: How testing and choice are undermining education.* New York, NY: Basic Books.

Smarter Balanced Assessment Consortium Common Core assessment. www.smarterbalanced.org

9

Differentiation

. . . more often than not, when students do not learn, they do not need "more"; rather, they need "different."

John Hattie, 2012, p. 93

Scenario
One Size Doesn't Fit All

Ms. Martinez was in her eleventh year of teaching and was well-respected by her peers, the administration, and the families alike. For the past seven years, she had been teaching third grade and loved working with this grade level. Despite her experience and love of teaching, Ms. Martinez felt that her job was getting more and more difficult. The students came into her class with great variations in academic, social, emotional, physical, and English development. The school had more and more English language learners, some of whom spoke languages like Somali, which she did not know. Response to Intervention (RTI) meant that all teachers needed to make greater efforts to meet the needs of students who were behind academically in the classroom before referring them for special programs.

Yet, all the students were expected to pass the same high-stakes reading and math tests at the end of the year. If they did not pass, they could take summer school and retake the test, but if they still didn't pass, they were held back in third grade. Although this didn't happen often, Ms. Martinez felt she had failed her students when they had to be held back, but she simply did not have enough time in the day to plan and teach separate lessons for all their different needs. One of the other third-grade teachers expressed some of the same concerns, but said she was trying some differentiation strategies that she had learned in a graduate class. These strategies allowed her to teach the same basic themes to everyone but make some modifications within the themes to meet the great diversity of needs.

Differentiation Strategies

Less is more ideas support differentiation. Students can be studying the same topic, but learn and express their knowledge in different ways. It "focuses on the quality of activities versus the quantity of work assigned" (Smith & Throne, 2007, p. 6). Differentiated instruction also works hand-in-hand with Response to Intervention (RTI) which attempts to intervene and meet students' individual needs in the mainstream classroom before they fail or fall significantly behind their peers.

There are dozens of strategies that can be used to differentiate instruction for all students, but we have chosen four to focus on here because they fit in well with *less is more* and integrated teaching. They are tiered activities, multiple modalities, technology, and centers. These are ideas that teachers can draw on to help them meet the needs of their students but they are not meant as "prescriptions" for every class. Rapid change can be stressful for teachers and students and often causes classroom management problems. For that reason, differentiation strategies should be introduced slowly to support teacher and student success.

Tiered Activities
Tiered activities involve all students learning about the same basic concepts, such as through integrated units, but with assignments that vary in difficulty based on student needs (Tomlinson, 1999). When teachers cover fewer topics, they have opportunities

to collect materials and design assignments at different difficulty levels. If grade-level teachers work together on creating the integrated units, the task of differentiating instruction within the units can become even easier.

Teachers should begin integrated units with whole-class instruction so everyone is introduced to the basic concepts of the unit together, which can be achieved through teacher read-alouds, online videos, graphic organizers, and other whole-class activities. After the introduction, the amount of structure and assistance provided to students can be adapted for varying needs. Some students may be able to move quickly to independent or small group work with little assistance from the teacher. Other students will need more structure and help. The teacher may break assignments into small parts, provide step-by-step instructions, monitor progress, and provide assistance frequently for students less prepared to work independently. It should be noted that the ability to work independently does not necessarily correlate with reading level or academic achievement. There are many good readers who have difficulty setting goals, maintaining attention, or completing open-ended assignments without teacher direction. Additional whole-class lessons should be provided as needed to introduce or reinforce concepts that are important to everyone in the class.

The selection of reading materials, including websites, is another way to modify instruction within a thematic unit. Reading materials vary in the use of academic vocabulary. In addition to vocabulary, the concreteness of the topics and their familiarity to the student are both factors in difficulty. For example, a text about the beach may be easier for students who have been to the beach than those who have not.

The pace and quantity of work also can be adjusted for different students. For example, a fourth-grade teacher might expect a recent immigrant with beginning English skills to write a two paragraph report while other students might be expected to write two or more pages.

There are a number of factors that can make assignments easier or more difficult that should be considered as lessons are adapted for students with different needs. The type of thinking and number of steps that students are expected to do during the assignment impacts complexity. For instance, an assignment that asks students to read one source and summarize it is much simpler than one that expects students to read numerous sources and synthesize the information. If applications are similar to those modeled in class, they will be easier than ones that require students to apply their knowledge and skills in totally new contexts.

Although the whole class will be learning about the same topic, tiered activities allow the teacher to adjust the materials, pace, quantity, and complexity of the assignments to better meet the diverse needs of students in the class. Story Retelling at the end of the chapter is an example of a tiered activity for the lower grades.

Multiple Modalities

Integrated units also provide numerous opportunities to tap different students' learning strengths. School usually focuses on learning through listening to the teacher and reading books, and demonstrating knowledge and skills through speaking and written responses, especially on tests. However, students can listen to videos and other students as well as the teacher. They can read songs, signs, texts, and computer websites as well as books. Students can dramatize what they have learned, create displays and explain them to other students, or interview family members to develop their speaking skills. They can write skits, emails, or illustrated books to practice their writing skills. Some students may learn about patterns through numbers, others through art, and still others through music and rhythm. A shy student may find it easier to speak through a puppet from the inside of a refrigerator box made into a puppet theater. Students who have trouble writing may be able to summarize a biography they read on a timeline that doesn't require extensive writing. Students who always seem to be challenging someone else's thinking could be encouraged to express their opinions supported by facts during a debate or in a persuasive letter.

As teachers plan integrated units, it is useful to think about the divergent ways that students learn and express themselves in order to differentiate instruction and assessment. Each lesson will not be able to accommodate all of these, but efforts should be made to use various instructional and assessment strategies throughout the year that tap into all students' strengths. The Outer Space activity at the end of the chapter incorporates multiple modalities as well as technology.

Use of Technology

Technology offers many opportunities for differentiation if it is used as a tool to support the ongoing curriculum rather than as an addition to the already overcrowded curriculum. One use of technology is to individualize learning. There are programs, tablets, websites, and apps where teachers and students can choose assignments based on needs and interests. The programs adapt the instruction as the student progresses, providing feedback for students and teachers, and review as needed.

Another use of technology is for research. The number of sites that are relatively safe and provide easy to understand information for elementary school children is growing. For example, www.iknowthat.com provides video and audio information so that even pre-kindergarteners can learn about issues that interest them.

In addition, technology can be used for communication purposes. Websites help students have their own blogs, contact authors or experts in a field, or write with pen pals around the world. Tips for blogging safely with youngsters are provided at www.kidslearntoblog.com and www.studentsoftheworld.info/menu_pres.html provides access to pen pals, blogs, and forums on a variety of topics for students. Creative endeavors can be encouraged through technology too. Composing music or designing buildings and fashion can now literally be done by a child on the computer.

Technology also can be used to assist students with disabilities. For example, a child who has trouble writing may be able to dictate ideas to the computer, which will type it for him and read it back, or the computer can enlarge type for a student who has trouble seeing.

Since most educational applications online, on computers or tablets, or on phones cost money, it is important for those purchasing the programs to think carefully about what they are buying. One thing to consider is whether the program supports the ongoing curriculum, especially the integrated units. The benefits of integrated units will be diluted if computer reading programs do not offer texts on the topics being studied. Most programs have free trials or demonstrations. Ideally, these should be tested with some of the students who will be using the program. One of the best sites to learn about games, apps, and websites for learning is www.graphite.org produced by Common Sense Media. This site is constantly updated, includes reviews of hundreds of educational programs, and is searchable for specific needs. For each product and website, graphite.org includes costs, grade levels, Common Core standards, set-up times, what type of hardware is needed, and reviews. In addition, the website provides links for more information about the searched product as well as links to competing products so teachers can compare products with similar goals. (Chapter 12 provides ideas on finding funding for technology.)

Centers

Centers are areas around the room with activities that extend learning. They provide many opportunities for differentiation and flexibility. The use of stations and/or centers allows teachers the freedom to walk around the room monitoring work and prompting students to extend their thinking. Once students understand what is expected of them at centers or stations, teachers also can pull aside one or more students for instruction specifically targeted to their needs.

Regardless of how centers are used in a particular classroom, there are general guidelines for making them successful. Students need to understand what is expected of them at each station or center, including what to do if they need help, what to do if they complete the activities, and how their work at the station or center will be recorded and/or evaluated. Centers and stations should have clear written instructions, which may include pictures for younger students. The teacher also should demonstrate how work will be done at each station or center before students begin working there.

For many teachers, stations and centers seem to be an overwhelming task. Again, this is an area where *less is more* applies. Teachers can begin with just one or two centers. A few students a day go to the centers and the rest of the students work individually or with partners at their desks. Everyone would have an opportunity to go to the centers at least once a week.

Another way to use *less is more* ideas is to keep some centers basically the same all year long. For example, a first-grade classroom could have a math center with ones, tens, and hundreds blocks all year long, but the assignments might change depending on the students at the center and the concepts that have been learned. Early in the year, the center might have students count using the ones sticks, trace the blocks onto paper, and write the numeral represented next to the drawing. Later in the year, the blocks could be used in a similar way to solve addition and subtraction problems. Students who finish the assigned problems early could write their own problems and solve them. Some students might be doing single digit addition or subtraction, while others are doing double or even triple digit problems. Volume Measurement at the end of the chapter provides ideas for a math center for upper elementary grade students.

Grading is another area where *less is more* is relevant. Although students should be responsible for completing work at all centers or stations, it is not necessary that they hand in a written assignment to be graded for each one. For example, fourth graders might keep a log of what poems they read at the poetry center and then choose one to respond to through writing or artwork, which could be shared with their peers at designated times, and students could place self-selected work in their portfolio. The poems available at the poetry center might change, but the center would remain the same all year.

Using tiered activities, varying teaching modalities, integrating technology, and setting up centers can go a long ways toward differentiating instruction for all types of students. In addition, special consideration should be given to differentiation for some groups of students.

Differentiation for Special Groups of Students

Differentiation for English Language Learners (ELLs)

The number of ELLs in the schools is growing and ELLs are found across the country, not just along the borders. Therefore, it is important for all teachers to be aware of ways to differentiate for ELLs.

For ELLs, teachers need to know not only the students' experience and knowledge in English but also in their native language. This makes an enormous difference when trying to plan instruction for ELLs. Some ELLs enter U.S. schools with extensive education in their native language, including reading, writing, math, and content area knowledge. These students don't need to learn to read all over again, especially if they already read in a language similar to English, such as Spanish. The emphasis of their instruction will be on learning English during integrated units and content area instruction. Other students enter school in the United States with little previous formal education in their native country due to poverty, war, or other upheaval. These students will probably need more instruction in the basics of reading or math in addition to learning the English language.

ELLs also differ in the support they receive at home. In some families, a parent, older sibling, or other relative may speak English and be able to help the student in their efforts to learn English while other families do not have English speakers. In addition, some families of ELLs are well-educated in their native lands and can provide content area support for their children in their native language even if they do not have extensive English skills. If the school has ELL teachers, they may be able to assist the mainstream classroom teacher in obtaining more detailed information about the students' backgrounds.

ELLs will benefit from strategies used to support differentiation for all students as well as some additional techniques. If possible, when students are working in pairs, place recent immigrants with other students who speak their native tongue but already have some English skills. In addition to working with others who speak their native language, ELLs should have many opportunities to work with native English speakers even if they mostly listen rather than talk at the beginning.

Learning English vocabulary is one of ELLs' primary learning tasks, and therefore, it is important to provide extra pictures, videos, body movements, and hands-on activities to support their English at the same time they are learning in the content areas. For example, if the class is doing a science experiment, the teacher may want to pick up or point to the items and name them so that the ELLs associate the words with the objects. Teachers may want to help ELLs create individual dictionaries, note cards, or file folders with words they want to learn that include pictures and/or translations into their native language.

Sometimes the abilities of ELLs are underestimated due to their lack of English vocabulary and assessments that are mostly in English. They may understand the concepts but be unable to express themselves in English. With ELLs, emphasis should always be placed on comprehension. When students are reading aloud or doing other oral activities, care must be taken to focus on the students' understanding of the task rather than their accents or grammar. ELLs only become proficient in English when they have many opportunities to use the language, even if it is not perfect. ELLs may be discouraged from using their English if they are afraid of being corrected (Maxwell, 2013).

It is also easy to overestimate students' knowledge of English. Conversational English develops before academic English so students may seem fluent in English when answering simple questions or speaking with friends, but they still may lack the academic English needed to succeed in the content areas. The academic language demands of the Common Core are higher than many traditional programs (Maxwell, 2013).

Differentiation for Specific Learning Needs

Differentiation is especially important for students with specific learning needs. Albert Einstein once said, "Insanity is doing the same thing over and over again and expecting different results." Yet, many students are forced to do drill and practice assignments over and over again in the mistaken belief that they need these skills to proceed to more complex tasks. Tomlinson and McTighe (2006) wrote, "It is not the case that struggling learners must master the basics before they can engage in thinking" (p. 8). Students often learn the basics by doing authentic activities, such as improving knowledge of letter sounds through actual reading.

Differentiation through Individualized Education Programs (IEPs) is required for students officially identified as having specific learning needs. The Common Core presents new challenges for educators developing IEPs (Samuels, 2013). However, special education experts believe the standards can be applied to special needs students if teachers look at the essence of the standards. For example, one of the standards expects students to be able to identify cause and effect in a story. Learning disabled students can learn to identify cause and effect, but they may need more concrete examples that relate closer to their lives. Even if they cannot read texts themselves, they can listen to text and respond to them orally or with pictures, thus allowing them to work on the same standards as the other students with modifications as needed.

Differentiation for Gifted and Talented Students

Many educators believe that students who are getting good grades and passing standardized tests do not need differentiation. However, successful students have special needs too. They need to be challenged rather than given more of the same type of work that they already have successfully completed. "When we work hard to understand information, we recall it better, the extra effort expended signals the brain that this knowledge is worth keeping" (Paul, 2013, para. 6).

In addition, many successful students are successful because they are good at following instructions and figuring out what the teacher or assessment wants, but they may not know how to set their own goals or monitor their own work. Gifted and talented learners need to be encouraged and prompted to become independent, self-regulated learners.

Gifted and talented students are often asked to help other students in the classroom, which can be helpful for the gifted student as well as the other students when done in moderation. When we teach someone else how to do something, we learn it better ourselves so the gifted student benefits from helping others. However, they do need their own challenging work as well. Also, not all gifted and talented students have the patience or personality to help other students.

The Common Core standards provide a framework for gifted and talented education because they require more critical thinking and problem solving, but teachers still need to differentiate within that framework. "While many educators feel that the common-core standards fall more in line with the pedagogy of gifted education than previous states' standards, the standards in and of themselves will not be sufficient to challenge a school's most advanced learners . . ." (Ash, 2013, p. S33).

Differentiation for Emotional and Social Needs

When educators are considering differentiation, they usually first think of academic needs, but differentiation also applies to social and emotional needs. Some students may have been identified with social and emotional needs, such as students with Autism or Attention Deficit Disorder while others may just not seem to be well adjusted in the classroom and still others may be going through temporary emotional stress due to problems at home. These students vary greatly but most benefit from clear written expectations with frequent oral reminders to the whole class and structured activities broken into small parts. Most students will benefit from lessons aimed at working better with others in the classroom. Special care should be taken when assigning these students to work with others. Although these students should be encouraged to interact with other students, requests to work alone should be honored.

Conclusion

Differentiation has always been a challenge for teachers but is even more so with high-stakes testing and the Common Core, which requires higher levels of critical thinking, reading, problem solving, and application of learning. "Designing such lessons for the typical student is tough enough for teachers; adapting them to children at wildly varied points on the skills spectrum is tougher still" (Gewertz, 2013, p. S4). The goal of this chapter was not to cover all methods of differentiation or suggest plans for specific students or classes, but rather to indicate that within integrated units, all students can be learning the same basic concepts with adaptations for their individual needs and interests. When educators teach fewer themes, they have the time to modify instruction within those themes. The following are more ideas about how instruction and assessments can be modified for individual needs.

Sample Lessons

Story Retelling

Participants: Kindergarten through first-grade students

Purpose: To provide different levels of support for story retelling within any theme on fictional literature.

Preparation: Practice story retelling activities as a class before doing this individual activity. Choose a picture story that has a clear sequence of events. Copy and shrink four or more pictures from the story and place them in random order on a sheet of paper and make copies for some of class. Write simple sentences representing important points in the story and put them in random order on a sheet of paper. Make copies for some of the class. Find a graphic organizer that allows students to fill in the important events in the story and copy for some of the class.

Activity Description
1. Read the story to the class.
2. Have students draw their favorite part of the story.
3. While students are drawing their favorite part of the story, call small groups of students aside and assign them one of the story retelling activities:
   a) Cut out pictures and glue them down in the correct order to retell the story to their partner.
   b) Cut out sentences and glue them down in the correct order to retell the story to their partner.

c) Complete the graphic organizer about the main events in the story to retell the story to their partner.
4. Monitor and prompt students as they work on their assignments.
5. Have students share their drawings and retelling activity with a partner.
6. Collect the retelling activities, grade, and provide individual feedback.

Common Core Reading Anchor 2: Determine central ideas or themes of a text and analyze their development; summarize the key supporting details and ideas.

Outer Space

Participants: First- through fifth-grade students

Purpose: To work with partners to successfully complete a research and presentation project. To use a variety of materials at different levels within an outer space theme.

Preparation: Conduct introductory activities for outer space unit. Preview videos, pictures, and games related to outer space at http://kids.nationalgeographic.com/kids/

Activity Description
1. Allow students to choose a place in outer space to study. Then place students with partners who want to investigate the same topic.
2. Provide students with a variety of sources of information, including access to National Geographic kids, which provides video, audio, and written information about outer space.
3. Students develop an advertisement explaining the highlights of their place for "potential visitors." They can include music, drawings, computer graphics, and writing in the advertisement.
4. Depending on the time available, have students present their advertisements to the whole class or to groups of other students from the class.

Common Core Reading Anchor 7: Integrate and evaluate content presented in diverse media and formats, including visually and quantitatively, as well as in words.

Writing Anchor 7: Conduct short as well as more sustained research projects based on focused questions, demonstrating understanding of the subject under investigation.

Volume Measurement

Participants: Fourth- through fifth-grade students

Purpose: Encourage students of different abilities to work together at a center to solve problems as part of a measurement theme.

Preparation: Collect a variety of rectangular prisms, cubes, and triangular prisms. There should be two of the same sized triangular prisms so students can see how they fit together to make a rectangular prism and discover that their volume is 1/2 their height x width x length. Number each figure so students can report on their findings. Provide rulers in the increments that you want them to measure (i.e., inches or centimeters or both). Start with figures that have whole number measurements, such as 4 cm x 8 cm x 3 cm.

Activity Description
1. After the class has worked on volume of cubes and rectangular prisms, introduce the center to the students.
2. Assign students to the center in heterogeneous groups. At first, have them measure and calculate the volume of each of the figures separately. Provide an answer sheet so they can check their answers. If they have incorrect answers, encourage them to discover where they made the mistake—with the formula for volume, the measurements, or the multiplication.
3. Then have students build houses or other creations with more than one block. Ask them to figure out the volume of these figures.
4. Monitor progress at the center. If students are having trouble determining the volume of a triangular prism, which is not a

requirement for fourth or fifth graders, place two of them together to make a rectangular prism and ask them what that means.

5. Add additional figures to the center with uneven measurements so that students have to multiply fractions in order to
calculate the volume.

Common Core: Fifth-Grade Overview—Understand concepts of volume
and relate volume to multiplication and to addition.

References

Ash, K. (2013). Gifted learners: Poised to 'join the conversation' in
moving beyond the mainstream: Helping diverse learners
master the common core. A special report on the Common
Core. *Education Week, 33*(10), S33–S34. Retrieved from www.
edweek.org/go/diverse-report

Gewertz, C. (2013). A Common Core for everyone in Moving beyond
the mainstream: Helping diverse learners master the common
core. A special report on the Common Core. *Education Week,
33*(10), S4–S6. Retrieved from www.edweek.org/go/diverse-report

Hattie, J. (2012). *Visible learning for teachers: Maximizing impact on
learning.* New York, NY: Routledge.

Maxwell, L. A. (2013). Language demands rise with Common Core in
Moving beyond the mainstream. Helping diverse learners
master the Common Core. A special report on the Common
Core. *Education Week, 33*(10), S14–S16. Retrieved from www.
edweek.org/go/diverse-report

Paul, A. M. (2013, September). When homework is a waste of time.
Time Magazine. Retrieved from http://ideas.time.com/2013/09/05/
when-homework-is-a-waste-of- time/

Samuels, C. A. (2013). Common Core's promise collides with IEP
realities in Moving beyond the mainstream. Helping diverse
learners master the Common Core. A special report on the
Common Core. *Education Week, 33*(10), S24–S25. Retrieved from
www.edweek.org/go/diverse-report

Smith, G. E., & Throne, S. (2007). *Differentiating instruction with
technology for K-5 classrooms.* Washington, D.C.: International
Society for Technology in Education.

Tomlinson, C. A. (1999). *The differentiated classroom: Responding to the needs of all learners.* Alexandria, VA: ASCD.

Tomlinson, C. A., & McTighe, J. (2006). *Integrating differentiated instruction + understanding by design.* Alexandria, VA: ASCD.

Other Resources

Apps, games, and websites for the classroom. www.graphite.org

Blogging with children. www.kidslearntoblog.com

Common Core for English language learners. www.colorincolorado. org/common-core/

Gardner, H. (1983). *Frames of mind: The theory of multiple intelligences.* New York, NY: Basic Books.

Gregory, G. H. (2003). *Differentiated instructional strategies in practice: Training, implementation, and supervision.* Thousand Oaks, CA: Corwin.

National Geographic for Kids. http://kids.nationalgeographic.com/kids/

Pen Pals. www.studentsoftheworld.info/menu_pres.html

Tomlinson, C. A. (1995). *How to differentiate instruction in mixed-ability classrooms.* Alexandria, VA: ASCD.

Websites for differentiating instruction retrieved from http://teaching. monster.com/benefits/articles/8484-using-technology-to-differentiate-instruction?page=1

Video and audio for children. www.iknowthat.com

10

Supporting Teachers Doing Less

Change is a process not an event.

Barbara Johnson

Scenario
Too Much to Do, So Little Time

Mr. Han, an instructional facilitator at Memorial Elementary School, brought in refreshments and met informally with teachers during some planning periods. During these meetings, he also made it a point to provide a variety of additional instructional resources based on teacher needs and requests. After years of doing this, the teachers trusted him and knew that he took their concerns seriously. For quite some time, he had been hearing complaints by even excellent teachers that they had too much material to cover and couldn't do it all justice. This was especially true since the state had adopted the Common Core standards that required more critical thinking in reading, writing, and problem solving. Teachers said their students didn't have time to do in-depth reading or revise and edit their writing. Often these discussions took place in the school's parking lot when teachers were leaving after a long day of work.

As he was looking for some possible solutions, Mr. Han came across the *less is more* ideas. He liked the idea of using about nine thematic units a year to reduce the amount that teachers felt they needed to cover. Although some math would need to be taught separately, almost all of the reading and language arts standards could be incorporated into the thematic units. Not only would students have time for real reading and writing, they would also be able to do research during the units, which was in the Common Core standards. Students also could collaborate and solve problems together as they worked on the units.

Mr. Han knew that if he was going to bring these ideas to the principal, Ms. Alexander, he would have to be able to show her how these ideas could be implemented at Memorial Elementary School. He began drawing up a plan to present to her.

Ms. Alexander had been principal at Memorial Elementary School for four years. Her relationship with Mr. Han and the teachers was solid. The faculty got along well with each other and she was confident that teachers liked and respected her. Generally, she felt good about the relationships in the school. Over time student achievement had remained steady and the parents and community seemed pleased with the school. She believed her teachers worked hard and were satisfied with the working conditions in the school as she had little turnover of staff. She tried to honor teachers' wishes for staff development and sought to provide as many resources as she could for the teachers.

Recently, Ms. Alexander had attended several meetings at the district level about the implementation of the new Common Core standards adopted by the state. Across the district, her principal colleagues had been discussing the impact of the new standards at their campuses and expressing concern as to how teachers were reacting to this mandate.

Change

The statistics on change reveal that 70 percent of all change efforts fail (Kotter, 2012). This statistic applies to schools too. Most educators have been through their share of numerous failed change efforts, i.e., elimination of report cards. They hope that if they wait long enough, proposed changes will go away and things will return to "normal." There is good reason teachers feel this way. Many change attempts are mandated from the top down with little to no input or buy in from teachers. Additionally, expert implementation of new initiatives is expected to happen quickly with few additional resources, professional development, or other ongoing support. Faculty who do wish to speak out and voice concerns about the intended changes are dismissed as negative. As a result, many excellent ideas about how to best support change efforts and overcome barriers are ignored.

Teachers facing the challenge of implementing change such as the new curriculum standards cannot be told to "just do it." Implementation of the new standards cannot become just one more thing forced on educators. Think of a Christmas tree if too many ornaments are added—the tree comes crashing down. We can't keep adding new programs and initiatives to schools without taking a few "ornaments" off. We don't want the tree [school] to topple over under the weight of add ons. Schools can do more better by doing less.

Continuous Improvement and Ongoing Implementation

School leaders play a key role in the implementation of new standards. Sorenson, Goldsmith, Mendez, and Maxwell (2011) place school leaders in the driver's seat when it comes to making curricular changes. They write, " . . . it is a principal's responsibility to effectively lead the change process if the expectation is an enhanced curriculum, continued organizational improvement, and increased student achievement." (p. 85). Principals' leadership of the curricular change process is central to success. However, teachers cannot be left out of the process.

Principals and teachers alike both play a critical leadership role in successful change. Hall and Hord (2011) note that change is a team effort. How teachers are involved in the implementation process matters greatly. Sullivan and Glanz write, "The way in which supervisors try to bring about change largely determines how teachers respond to the challenge. Supervisors can mandate change externally; or they can, together with teachers, build collaborative cultures that encourage the seeds of change to take root and grow" (2013, p. 118).

Collaborative cultures in schools can be nurtured and developed. An important beginning step in building this type of culture is to assess the current level of teacher collaboration by examining the quality of adult relationships in the school. Adult relationships are a key factor in allowing schools to improve and change (Barth, 2006). Healthy adult relationships are necessary for school improvement and change. The likelihood of successful change improves when adult relationships get healthier and stronger.

Barth (2006) categorizes four types of adult relationships in schools: parallel play, adversarial, congenial, and collegial. Of the four types of relationships, congenial and collegial are key to building collaborative cultures. Collegial and congenial relationships stand in stark contrast to parallel play and adversarial relationships that lead to a culture of teacher isolation and competition. In schools in which adults are engaged in parallel play, teachers work in isolation alongside each other with no intention or plan to share ideas or tools to improve coworkers' teaching practices. Schools with adversarial teacher relationships have a competitive culture in which teachers intentionally withhold valuable information about professional practice from one another. Teachers compete with one another to be recognized as the "best" and "fight" for limited resources.

Congenial adult relationships are found in collaborative school cultures. Barth states, "We all see evidence of congeniality in schools. A lot of it seems to center around food: One teacher makes the coffee and pours it for a colleague. Or around the activities of daily living: A principal gives a teacher a ride home so she can care for her sick child. Congenial relationships are personal and friendly" (2006, p. 11).

Congenial adult relationships are an essential and necessary ingredient for the most important type of adult relationships in a school, collegiality. A school that is going to be truly successful in the full implementation of the Common Core standards or other curricular changes needs to have collegiality. Collegiality is noted by Barth (2006) to be amongst the hardest adult relationships to establish in a school. Barth describes such relationships as, ". . . getting them [teachers] to play together, about growing a professional learning community" (p. 10).

Professional learning communities (PLCs) provide the framework for increased collaboration amongst teachers (Hord, 1997). They are not something new to be added on to existing programs. Rather they are the way professionals work with and learn from one another to build the instructional capacity of a school. PLCs provide the intentional structure that brings teachers together to share ideas, materials, and resources, model instructional strategies, identify student learning goals, examine student work, analyze data, and above all examine teacher impact on student achievement. Opportunities for collaboration and collective learning are the support needed by teachers for the successful implementation of curricular changes. Teachers cannot be expected to significantly change their practices in isolation without the support of collaborative colleagues. PLCs help change "take root and grow."

Killion and Hirsh write, "To achieve the results promised in Common Core standards, states, districts and school leaders must make smart and new investments in the capacity of educators" (2013, p. 14). PLCs are such an investment. They have the potential to build the collective capacity of teachers in a school to increase student learning. Hattie writes, ". . . the greatest effects on student learning occur when teachers become learners of their own teaching . . ." (2012, p. 18). He further notes, ". . . teachers themselves need to be in a safe environment to learn about success, or otherwise of their teaching from others" (p. 19). PLCs provide this safe environment for teachers to critically examine their impact on student learning, take risks and learn how to get better.

Schools like Memorial Elementary School in our opening scenario can provide a supportive teacher environment for the ongoing implementation of new standards through the development of a PLC. PLCs change the way teachers "do business" with one another. However, faculty should be in agreement about their school developing into a PLC. PLCs can't be forced.

Several *less is more* lessons can be applied.

TABLE 10.1 Building a Collegial Teacher Culture to Support Change

DO LESS	DO MORE
Less rush to change	More assessment of organizational readiness
Less top-down decision making	More teacher empowerment
Less isolation of faculty and staff	More intentional collaboration between faculty and staff
Less competition over resources and withholding of professional practices	More intentional sharing of successful instructional practices and resources
Less Me	More We (team approach)
Less distrust of teachers' ideas and viewpoints	More confidence in teacher professionalism
Less adding of competitive initiatives	More focus on teacher learning through PLCs.
Less individual learning	More collective learning

Supporting Teachers in Curriculum Integration of the Common Core Standards

School district efforts to build awareness about the Common Core standards are informative, but often lack the support needed to help teachers adjust the curriculum and transform classroom practice. The Common Core Implementation Checklist published by the National Association of Elementary School Principals identifies critical steps for principals to take in preparation for the implementation of the Common Core. (*The authors realize that some schools are beyond these steps. Nevertheless schools further along in the implementation process may wish to review them.*)

A sampling of the questions on the checklist include: "Are you exploring ways to implement the Common Core standards? Are teachers taking small steps to adjust rigor and expectations? Are you facilitating understanding of curriculum changes for math? Are you identifying grade levels/subjects that might need more help in implementing the Common Core in your school? And are adjustments in curriculum needed (which areas/grades)?" ("Common Core Implementation Checklist," 2013). At first glance, the checklist questions seem overwhelming for both school leaders and teachers alike. Unless you are a PLC. Most educators will be very receptive to the idea of a PLC, which provides opportunities to dialogue about and work through these issues as a group. Educators should not feel isolated and alone as they move forward with the implementation of the Common Core standards or any other changes.

Teachers overcome with frustration about the amount of material to be covered and the increased rigor of the Common Core standards should be introduced to and encouraged to implement the *less is more* concept of curriculum integration. This approach encourages teachers to work together to combine topics, cut out repetition, and provide students with more time to delve into topics. It is an approach to help adjust a school's curriculum to meet the expectations for increased student learning.

In order for curriculum integration to work, teachers must engage in collaborative planning. Together, the school faculty must reach consensus on what topics to cover at each grade level and what topics to cut. Grade-level teams need to outline units based on selected topics and develop lessons that support the increased learning expectations for students. Teachers also may need to identify additional resources and materials, i.e., more nonfiction texts. Beyond planning, teachers must collaboratively examine how their integrated lessons impact student learning and what instructional changes are needed to increase teacher effectiveness. PLCs intentionally create the opportunities for teachers to have this much needed dialogue. They have the potential to provide all teachers and school leaders the support needed to successfully implement the Common Core standards.

Initiating a Professional Learning Community

A comprehensive discussion on how to form a PLC is beyond the scope of the book. However, the authors have identified five areas they regard as important in getting started with a PLC. (1) Decisions need to be made about how collaborative teams are formed or structured across the school. (2) A cadre of teacher leaders need to be identified who would help facilitate collaborative PLC meetings. (3) Skills need to be identified that support teachers in becoming members of collaborative and productive teams including establishing norms for operation. (4) Protocols or procedures need to be established to help focus teacher meetings on important issues. And (5) Schools must find time for collaboration. (*It is assumed that school leaders have already assessed the quality of adult relationships in the school when moving forward with a PLC.*)

Team Structure and Leadership

Many elementary schools have grade-level teams with one specific teacher designated as a team leader. Each grade-level team can function as its own learning community with the teacher leader serving as the facilitator. This cadre of grade-level leaders can also meet as a community of learners to ensure schoolwide alignment of goals. Team structure decisions also should include which learning communities will be joined by professionals who serve multiple grade levels. These professionals include librarians, counselors, fine arts teachers, physical education teachers, etc.

Learning to Be Collaborative

A common mistake in the implementation of PLCs is overlooking the need to support teachers with the skills to collaboratively work in a group. Thessin and Starr (2011) write "Teachers do not magically know how to work with colleagues; districts must support and lead that work if PLCs are to live up to their potential" (p. 49). Principals must ensure that teacher leaders have the skills necessary to facilitate PLCs. These facilitation skills include utilizing protocols to guide focused team discussions on critical topics, i.e., curriculum integration, and helping teachers learn the roles, responsibilities, and norms for working together in a productive group. School leaders cannot assume that teachers possess these skills or will learn them on their own. Specific opportunities must be provided for teachers and teacher leaders to learn and develop these collaborative group skills.

The authors of this text like the concept of the Critical Friends Group as a pathway or model for creating productive teacher work groups. The model supports teachers by furnishing them with specific skills and tools to work collaboratively as a PLC. The Critical Friends Group was initially developed by the Annenberg Institute for School Reform at Brown University as a model for collegial dialogue. The School Reform initiative website describes the Critical Friends Group as, "an intentional professional learning community dedicated to improving teaching and learning through collaboration, reflective dialogue . . ." (Thompson-Grove, Thierer, & Hensley, 2008, para. 2).

The Critical Friends Group model provides targeted training for teacher leaders to learn to facilitate PLC meetings. The National School Reform Faculty which hosts the Critical Friends Group website specifies the skills leaders or coaches will develop through the training. The skills include, "setting norms for working together, active listening, understanding guidelines for dialogue, understanding the dynamics of offering and receiving warm (supportive) or cool feedback, formulating clarifying and probing questions and using protocols for examining student and teacher work . . ." (National School Reform Faculty, 2012, para. 15).

In addition to providing skills training, a variety of established protocols or guidelines for focused conversations are readily available from the Critical Friends Group. This eliminates the need for leaders to develop their own. Furnishing teachers with the tools to be collaborative is essential. Meetings must be intentional and productive, otherwise time set aside for collaboration becomes a waste of time and the capacity for collective learning is diminished. Collaborative meetings have tangible outcomes.

Providing supportive conditions is an important attribute or dimension of a PLC. Hord writes, "Supportive conditions determine *when* and *where* and *how* the staff regularly come together as a unit to do the learning, decision making, problem solving and creative work that characterizes a professional learning community" (1997, p. 20). Two types of conditions are needed to support professional learning communities: the physical structure such as time and resources and the human qualities or capacities of teachers. Providing teachers with the tools and skills for collaboration and healthy relationships between adults deals with the human qualities aspect of PLCs.

Finding Time

Creating structures and schedules and finding time that allows for teacher collaboration is an important part of the supportive physical condition needed for PLCs (Hord, 1997). Over 20 years ago, Raywid wrote, "Ask anybody directly involved in school reform about its most essential ingredient, and the answer is likely to be 'time'" (1993, p. 30).

Today's schools still continue to struggle with finding time for collaboration. Most recently the authors heard of a local school struggling to raise test scores that is designating Sundays as a teacher meeting day! Requiring that teachers add *more* time into their busy and long weeks is not the answer to finding time for teacher collaboration. The authors recommend less meeting time outside the school day and weekends and more collaborative time within teachers' regular work day. Adding time within a teacher's regular workday is very difficult given the widely held view by many (politicians, parents, administrators) that teachers' time is best spent in direct contact with students. Finding time for teacher collaboration cannot be viewed as a bonus or luxury. It must be viewed an essential ingredient to build teachers' instructional capacity to improve student achievement (Killion & Hirsh, 2013; Darling-Hammond,1999). Professional learning must be continuous and ongoing to support and sustain school improvement/change.

Finding time is not the same as adding time. Time is found by assessing how well a school currently uses time and examining possibilities for restructuring it. The edited book, *Finding Time for Professional Learning* (von Frank, 2008) is a compilation of articles for schools seeking ideas on how to find more collaboration time for teachers. Ideas include:

- ◆ Combine teacher planning periods with non-instructional time such as lunch and after school.
- ◆ Blend students at a particular grade level into one group for special classes such as art, music, and physical education to make time for teachers to meet.

- Center faculty meetings around teacher learning rather than announcements that can be sent via email or written memo.
- Lengthen the school day four days a week (Monday—Thursday) by several minutes to allow for an early release day of students on the fifth day, Friday.
- Schedule common planning time for teachers at a particular grade level. For example, all first-grade teachers would be off at the same time.
- Hire substitute teachers to take over teachers' classrooms to make time for teacher planning and collaboration.
- Make video tapes of model lessons to share with colleagues for viewing at convenient times.
- Provide online discussion groups which serve as professional communities where teachers can discuss ideas and issues.
- Identify teacher in-service days on the school calendar and designate them as collaborative work sessions as opposed to traditional "sit and get" sessions.
- Find paraprofessionals and or educational interns that can provide instruction to students to free up teachers for planning.
- Use federal funds, i.e., Title One, to hire part-time teachers that can manage classes and provide instruction to provide time for teacher collaboration.

Looking at the Special Education literature on co-planning also provides ideas for finding time. One such idea is to use substitute teacher planning time (Stetson). Every day the school can create a calendar of all the substitute teachers in the building and their assigned planning periods. During the planning periods the substitutes report to the office to be assigned to a specific teacher's classroom to free teachers up for collaboration or peer observations. Teachers can choose to accept the planning time or not depending on the day's activities or lesson difficulty.

Sparks (2008) suggests that schools wanting more time for professional learning begin by selecting the "finding time" strategy they want to try and then identify 10 percent of the teacher's work time or three to four hours a week for collaboration with the restructured time. Starting small allows schools to experiment and take risks with restructuring time to find what works in their setting. As schools develop into stronger and more collaborative PLCs, teachers will become more skilled at using their time productively. Many (2009) writes, "Teachers find they need less time learning about the work and more time working on the work" (p. 8).

Teachers can be supported in doing less by developing schools into PLCs and encouraging the use of curriculum integration. Change will not only be initiated; it will be sustained. "What change is really about is people and their implementation of new practices in their classrooms, schools, school districts and states" (Hall and Hord, 2011, p. 27).

Activities to Support Change

Researching Finding Time Strategies

Participants: Teachers and teacher leaders, school leaders

Purpose: To explore various strategies as to how schools can find time for teacher collaboration.

Preparation: Make copies of an article on finding time. See reference section for possible articles, i.e., Many's article titled "Make Time for Collaboration." Photocopies of this chapter's section on Finding Time may also be used.

Activity Description

1. The school principal will distribute an article on how to make time for teacher collaboration to teacher leaders for reading.
2. Team leaders will next discuss the article or chapter with their respective grade-level teams. Each team will be asked to reflect upon the strategies and select one or two strategies that they think may work for their grade level and/or school-wide.

3. Each team leader will prepare a summary of their grade-level team's responses to share in a face-to-face meeting of all grade-level team leaders.
4. Team leaders will come together and share the summary of their grade-level team's discussion with the intent of selecting one to two strategies that the school would be willing to implement in an effort to find time for collaboration.
5. School leaders will facilitate the team leader discussion and decision of the finding time strategies that will be implemented school-wide.

Extension: Strategies selected may require approval from the district superintendent and/or school community or additional funds. Team leaders' discussion may identify the additional approvals needed and plan to take the appropriate action.

Minefield—Team-Building Exercise

Participants: All faculty, staff, and administrators on a campus divided into pairs

Purpose: To work on healthy relationships and build trust amongst pairs or teams of teachers.

Preparation: Find a list of team-building activities and select one to use with teams at the start of a faculty meeting or professional development session. An example of trust-building activities can be retrieved online from various sites such as: www.onlineexpert.com/elearning/user/pdf/NatSem/ManagingDiverseWorkforce/Team-BuildingGamesActivities Ideas.pdf. A favorite activity of the authors is Mine Field, retrieved online from www.huddle.com/blog/team-building-exercises/

Activity Description
1. Identify a school counselor or teacher leader who will be willing to facilitate this trust building activity.

2. Identify a 20–30 minute session in which all teachers will be in attendance to conduct this team building activity, i.e., faculty meeting or professional development session.
3. Prepare materials needed by printing copies of directions for the Mine Field Exercise and setting up an indoor space such as a gym or outdoor space as a parking lot filled with "mines" and blindfolds.
4. Conduct the activity with the faculty and reflect upon its results afterwards.

Extension: Although the activity is designed to be done in pairs the team size may be increased to sizes of four or five and selecting the winning team based on the time it takes to navigate each member one at a time through the "mine field." As each team member finishes he or she may join the leader in giving directions to the remaining team members who must navigate the "mine field" safely. The team which gets the most members through the mine field safely and the fastest wins.

References

Barth, R. (2006). Improving relationships in the schoolhouse. *Educational Leadership, 63*(6), 8–13.

Common Core Implementation Checklist (2013). National Association of Elementary School Principals. Retrieved from www.naesp.org/sites/default/files/common%20core%20checklist_2_22_201 3as.pdf

Darling-Hammond, L. (1999). Target time toward teachers. *Journal of Staff Development, 20*(2), 31–36.

Hall, G., & Hord, S. (2011). *Implementing change patterns, principles and potholes.* Boston, MA: Pearson.

Hattie, J. (2012). *Visible learning for teachers: Maximizing impact on learning.* New York, NY: Routledge.

Hord, S. (1997). Professional Learning Communities: Communities of continual inquiry and improvement. Southwest Educational Development Laboratory. Retrieved from www.sedl.org/pubs/change34/plc-cha34.pdf

Killion, J., & Hirsh, S. (2013). Investments in professional learning must change. *Journal of Staff Development, 34*(4), 10–20.

Kotter, J. (2012). *The 8-step process for leading change.* Retrieved from www.kotterinternational.com/kotterprinciples/changesteps

Many, T.W. (2009, May/June). Make time for collaboration. *Texas Elementary Principals and Supervisors Association News,* 8–9. Retrieved from www.allthingsplc.info/files/uploads/make_time_for_collaboration.pdf

National School Reform Faculty (2012, August 13). Frequently asked questions. Retrieved from www.nsrfharmony.org/faq.html

Raywid, M. A. (1993). Finding time for collaboration. *Educational Leadership, 51*(1), 30–34.

Sorenson, R., Goldsmith, L .M., Mendez, L., & Maxwell, K.T. (2011). *The Principal's guide to curriculum leadership.* Thousand Oaks, CA: Corwin.

Sparks, D. (2008). How can schools make time for teacher learning? In V. von Frank (Ed.), *Finding TIME for Professional Learning* (p. 32). Oxford, OH: National Staff Development Council. (Original work published 1999).

Stetson, F. Finding time for collaboration and using it well. *Inclusive Schools Network Houston.* Retrieved from http://inclusiveschools.org/finding-time-for-collaboration-and-using-it-well/

Sullivan, S., & Glanz, J. (2013). *Supervision that improves teaching: Strategies and techniques.* Thousand Oaks, CA: Corwin.

Thessin, R.A., & Starr, J.P. (2011). Supporting the growth of effective Professional Learning Communities. *Phi Delta Kappan, 9*(6), 48–54.

Thompson-Grove, G., Thierer, K., & Hensley, F. (2008). *A history of the school reform initiative.* Retrieved from www.schoolreforminitiative.org/pages/

von Frank, V. (Ed.). (2008). *Finding TIME for professional learning.* Oxford, OH: National Staff Development Council.

Other Resources
Combes, J., Edmonson, S., & Harris, S. (2013). *The trust factor: Strategies for school leaders.* New York, NY: Routledge.

Haar, J., & Ford, K. (2008). *Professional learning communities: An implementation guide and toolkit.* New York, NY: Routledge.

Team-Building Exercises. www.huddle.com/blog/team-building-exercises/

Trust-Building Exercises. www.onlineexpert.com/elearning/user/pdf/NatSem/ManagingDiverseWorkforce/Team-BuildingGames ActivitiesIdeas.pdf

11

Families, Communities, and Schools Working Together

True communication occurs when parents and teachers strive for a meaningful exchange around topics that affect children's learning.

Gaitan, 2004, p. 23

Scenario
Families and Change

Ms. Johnston, the principal at Central Elementary School, sat in her office after a productive meeting with teachers, trying to decide what to do next. The teachers and administrators at Central had decided over the last couple months that they wanted to adopt the ideas of *less is more*, especially trying to reduce the breadth of the curriculum and increase the depth of student learning. They all realized that teachers were going to need more time to collaborate with other teachers, not only from their own grade levels but also from other grade levels. Today the teachers had decided the best way to do this was to extend the school day by 15 minutes four days of the week and let school out an hour early on Wednesdays so they could collaborate from 2:30 to 4:30 pm once a week without disturbances or having to plan for a substitute teacher.

Ms. Johnston liked this idea and thought bus schedules and other concerns could be worked out, but she worried about the reaction from the families. She remembered when a previous superintendent had decided to institute a year-round school schedule. It had seemed like such a good idea, reducing the normal learning loss that occurs during summer breaks. Although students no longer had long summer breaks, they had more frequent short breaks during the year. Families complained bitterly about all the problems they encountered finding day care during intersessions. After only one year, the school board removed the superintendent, who had implemented the year-round school schedule, and the district went back to a traditional schedule. Although Central was not planning anything that drastic, Ms. Johnston wanted to make sure families were part of the change from the beginning.

She started to make a list of things to do to involve families and the community in the proposed change. Ms. Johnston decided to schedule a series of meetings at various times during the week to explain the possible changes to families and give them an opportunity to ask questions, express concerns, and offer suggestions. They would need to have meetings in English, Spanish, and Tagalog, the predominant languages spoken in the community. The meetings would be announced on the school website, notes home in the three languages, and through the media. Maybe the PTA could help to get the word out and even sponsor some of the meetings with refreshments. The more she thought, the more ideas she had. Some of the community churches and the Boys and Girls Club already offered after school programs; she was going to talk with them to see if they could start an hour earlier on Wednesdays. They might have other ideas too and could help communicate the potential changes to the local families. Ms. Johnston knew this proposed schedule change was not going to happen quickly, but she was now confident that it would go smoothly once the families saw that their needs were being considered.

Communication

Communicating with families is always important, but it becomes even more vital during times of school change as with *less is more* or Common Core. Most people can handle change if they are prepared for it, but don't appreciate getting last minute notices about changes when the school has been aware of the plans for a long time. Communicating before changes are made takes longer, but builds trust and relationships that will help later if there are setbacks or unexpected consequences of the change process.

Although some communication may be one way, such as notices on a website or newsletters that are sent home once a month, families need to have many opportunities to participate in two-way communication, including surveys, conferences with teachers, open-meetings, or special events, such as breakfasts where the changes are discussed. An example of this is the Common Core State Standards Family Night explained at the end of the chapter.

Most children speak English fluently by the upper grades but that doesn't mean their caregivers are fluent in English, and the students shouldn't be depended upon to translate for their families. Therefore, both written and oral communication should consider the languages of the families at the school (Rubin, Abrego, & Sutterby, 2012).

Ms. Johnston, in the scenario at the beginning of the chapter, realized that the teachers at her school would soon be having parent conferences either in person or over the phone concerning report cards and asked them to discuss the possible schedule changes with the families and jot down the families' questions, concerns, and suggestions. The teachers would then bring these to the next faculty meeting and some of them could be addressed on the website and in the monthly newsletter. This would show those families who had questions, concerns, or suggestions that their ideas were valued and would help to answer questions for other families who might have similar ideas but didn't express them during the report card conference.

Just as the languages and cultures of families differ so do their modes of communication. Some prefer more personal face-to-face communication while others find email or other electronic means much more convenient. Some families depend on other families at the school for much of their information. The Families to Families example at the end of the chapter provides ideas on how schools can capitalize on these informal communication networks. It is important that schools do not depend on only one means of communication, such as a school website, to communicate important changes with families and the community.

What Is the Change?

Almost all families want the best education possible for their children, even if they express it in different ways. Therefore, it is vital to explain to them how changes are going to improve the education of their children. For example, a school that uses *less is more* will most likely have fewer graded papers going home. Students will be doing longer assignments rather than more numerous short assignments, and teachers will be providing more feedback while students are working rather than taking stacks of papers home, grading them, and handing them back. For families, the important message is that they may see fewer graded papers, but this actually reflects an improvement in their child's education. Educators can explain that the students will be doing assignments that will better prepare them for high school, higher education, and jobs. For example, instead of doing many reading worksheets, they will be reading more real texts, including books, Internet sites designed for children, and pamphlets from local agencies about relevant topics, such as nutrition. Far better that this is discussed before changes are made than having families coming to the school and complaining that their child's teacher is no longer teaching because they are not seeing as many graded papers.

Similar considerations should be made with the Common Core standards. Families need to know how the Common Core differs from the previous standards and curriculum. For example, the Common Core places greater emphasis on thinking skills and reading informational text than most previous standards, but it does not require the use of specific books or programs as some families believe. It sets goals for students but does not specify how teachers should help students reach those goals.

What Does It Mean?

We once surveyed families of young children who were participating in an after-school program about what they would like to learn more about and were surprised to learn the answer was the major assessments that were given in kindergarten through second grade before the high-stakes testing began in third grade. Looking back, we shouldn't have been surprised that grading and assessment are two of the major concerns of families. The families wanted to learn about what was being assessed, for example—what was phonemic awareness? They wanted to learn how to read the reports that were sent home to them. What did each score mean? Was this a norm-referenced assessment in which a 50 percent meant that their child had done average? Or was this a criterion-referenced assessment in which a 50 percent meant that they had failed, only knowing half of the material on the test? Had the content on a mid-year assessment already been taught or was this a benchmark measuring what students should know by the end of the year? Most important, what did the scores mean for their child's future? Did their child need extra help? Would this information be used to hold their child back a grade? Could their child retake the assessment after receiving assistance in the trouble area? Should they do something differently at home?

Reports cards also need to be clarified for many families (Deslandes & Rivard, 2013). *Less is more* calls for more differentiation in instruction, which means that children will be working at their own level, trying to reach grade level or beyond by the end of the year. It is important that this is explained to families, especially of those children who are working below grade level. Families need to understand that their child is being given below-grade-level work in order to give them successful experiences, which they might not currently have if they were only working in grade-level materials. The teacher needs to explain that he still has high expectations for that child and will do everything possible to bridge the gap between the child's current level and grade-level work. Specific steps, such as after-school or weekend programs, should also be discussed. If the child is receiving grades based on below-grade-level work, this also should be examined. A "B" on second-grade work for a fourth grader is not the same as a "B" on fourth-grade-level work. Many families have complained when their child has received good grades throughout the school year and is suddenly referred for summer school, special education, or even retention at the end of the year, because the child was working on below-grade-level materials without their knowledge. These types of surprises can be avoided by having good communication throughout the school year. Most families will also want to know what they can do at home to help their child, which brings us to our next section.

What Can Families Do to Help Their Children?

Most families would like to support their children's education but are not sure about the best ways to help. Traditionally, the way families have helped children at home is through their homework. However, *less is more* calls for much less homework because it does not improve students' achievement or learning at the elementary school level (Hattie, 2012). Instead of homework, families should be provided with developmentally appropriate activities that they can do at home to help their children on a regular basis, such as reading aloud to their children in their home language, involving their children in chores and hobbies, talking with their children about TV shows or other daily activities, and asking their children questions about what they are reading or writing about at school. If homework will be given occasionally, this should be explained to the families. For example, teachers may want to send home a note at the beginning of each thematic unit telling the families what they will be studying and asking them to help their child find items, take or draw pictures, or even help locate speakers who could help them with the thematic unit. I did this with a second-grade unit on Native Americans while teaching at a school that included numerous Native American children. The response was unbelievable, including one field trip to see pictographs and another walking trip with a tribe elder near the school to explore native plants and how they can be used. Needless to say, the students were not the only ones who learned.

Slowing Down

Part of *less is more* is slowing down, especially when making curricular and assessment changes. One of the concerns people have encountered with the Common Core is the speed at which it has been implemented. Perhaps more important than implementation of the standards is assessment based on the new standards. It takes years for the new curricular changes to be fully implemented and for students to reap the benefits of the standards. New York state, which was one of the first to implement assessments based on the new standards, has faced a backlash from families, some of whom even boycotted the exams (Hernandez & Baker, 2013). Only 31 percent of students in third through fifth grades in New York state passed the 2013 exams. Many educators believe they simply did not have time for the professional development, planning, and teaching that was necessary for most students to succeed on the new tests, which emphasize critical thinking, analysis, and problem solving more than previous assessments (Hernandez & Gebeloff, 2013). Most states field-tested Common Core assessments in the spring of 2014 to prepare for the real assessments during the 2014–2015 school year (Minnich, 2014).

Ongoing Interactions

Many times families are involved at the beginning of the change process. They may attend meetings and be provided with information about impending changes. Some families may even be involved in the decision-making process. However, this is not enough. Families need to have an active ongoing role in any change process for it to be successful. New families have children entering the school district, modifications are made during the implementation of change, and challenges that may not have been apparent at the beginning become visible.

For example, most people, including families with children in elementary school, supported No Child Left Behind at the beginning of the implementation process. No one wants children to be left behind. Standardized testing sounded like a good idea to force teachers and schools to be accountable and make sure that students, who have not mastered basic skills, are not promoted from grade to grade without extra assistance. However, after families realized the impact of the standardized testing on their children, they began to question the assessments and the way the results were being used.

Conclusion

Therefore, it is not only important to listen to families' concerns and suggestions when *less is more* is first being adopted but throughout the undertaking. Although teachers are the experts in education, families know their children best. When changes are made with little or no communication with families, barriers develop between the families and schools, even leading to the opening of competing schools. By listening to families and acting on reasonable suggestions, schools indicate that they value the families' input and are flexible enough throughout the process to make modifications that will increase opportunities for student success. The following are examples of ways that schools can successfully engage families.

Family and Community Activities

Common Core State Standards Family Night

Purpose: The purpose of this activity is to help acquaint adult family members with the factual information regarding the Common Core State Standards (CCSS). Note this activity is designed for states who have adopted the CCSS. However, the activity could be modified using one's own state standards for states not adopting the CCSS.

Participants: School faculty and adult family members. (Students may come to school with their families, but a separate activity should be planned for them; children's movie night, read aloud in the library, arts and crafts, etc. High school students, Boys and Girls Clubs, or other community organizations may be able to assist with conducting these activities.)

Preparation: School faculty should meet to plan and organize the CCSS family night. At the initial planning meeting, faculty need to make decisions on the content and the type of interactive format to be used to acquaint family members with the CCSS. It is important that the materials are prepared in home languages as needed for the school community.

A site such as www.corestandards.org/ provides a variety of possible ideas. For example, this site includes topics such as "what parents should know" and "myths vs. facts." The limitation with this site is that it is English only.

Other sites such as the National PTA site provide parent guides entitled *Parents' Guide to Student Success* in Spanish and English; and the Louisiana Department of Education's site provides links to the PTA guide in Arabic and Vietnamese: www.louisianabelieves.com/resources/ library/family-support-toolbox-library. The PTA guides are organized by grade level for grades 1–8. They provide an overview of math and English Language Arts/Literacy CCSS that students at the grade level will be working on as well as ideas for talking to teachers about academic progress and helping children learn at home.

Websites such as Colorín Colorado have a specific section devoted to parent information on the CCSS in multiple languages: www.color incolorado.org/common-core/parents/languages/

Once the decision has been made as to the materials needed and format of the session, materials will need to be printed in the appropriate languages and/or the appropriate number of computers or mobile devices set up for Internet access. It is strongly suggested that teachers decide on key talking points in advance so that parents are able to obtain the information they need and want. Students may prepare the invitations for their families in their home language. If possible, let students write or illustrate the note being sent home.

Description of Activity: Schools will select a date and time to hold their CCSS family night and prepare and send invitations. Schools may wish to do this activity school-wide or by grade level. If possible, these authors recommend hosting by grade level on different nights so that families with students at more than one grade level can attend.

1. Children attending the event will report to a large location such as a gym, library, or cafeteria for their own activity such as a movie night.

2. Adult family members will go to a separate location in which they will be given the opportunity to explore the CCSS by grade level. If a school-wide event is hosted, parents may go to separate classrooms based on their child's grade. If a grade-level event is hosted, parents may meet in one location given the smaller number in attendance.

3. At the meeting, parents will be given an overview of the CCSS and an opportunity to explore the grade-level standards and sample student assignments. Materials may be in hard copy in home languages or located online as appropriate for the school demographics.

4. Parents who may have further questions concerning the standards may sign up to meet with school personnel in person at a later date or to be contacted by phone or email.

Families to Families

Purpose: Most families speak to other families about school issues, but some of the information distributed is incorrect. The purpose of this activity is to take advantage of these informal family networks to communicate important and accurate information to families and to receive feedback from families.

Participants: Volunteer family members from various language and cultural backgrounds

Preparation: Recruit family members from various language and cultural backgrounds who are willing to act as contact people in the community. Provide an orientation in which these family members learn about the type of activity you would like them to do (i.e., hand out flyers), where you would like them to do it (i.e., outside local grocery stores), and the answers to questions they are likely to be asked. More preparation will be needed if they are going to be asked to do presentations for local groups. They also should be provided with contact information for people at the school who can answer additional questions.

Description of Activity: The following are ways that well-informed family members can be used to communicate information to other families about changes or intended changes. Information can be distributed door-to-door, at grocery stores, churches, parks, and other gathering places for families of children at the school. Some families are also willing to host small informational gatherings in their home. All volunteers should be provided with cards with the names, phone numbers, and email of people at the school who can answer questions they are unable to answer.

1. Talk to other families in their home language about upcoming meetings where important issues will be discussed.
2. Hand out written information, prepared by the school in the families' home language, and be available to answer questions.
3. Present PowerPoint or other presentations, prepared by the school, at meetings of interested groups.
4. Help with booths at local fairs or events that local families attend.
5. Interview or pass out surveys to other families to gain feedback from families, especially those who may not participate in more traditional communication networks.

Community Outreach

Purpose: To gain community support for proposed changes and resources needed for changes.

Participants: Community leaders

Preparation: Identify appropriate community leaders in the area served by the school. The leaders may vary from project to project but could include leaders from business, government, religious organizations, service organizations, community centers, youth organizations, and media.

Description of Activity: The following are a few of the possible ways that community outreach can help schools communicate about change and obtain needed resources.

1. Contact businesses for donations of older computers, printers, and other technology that still works.
2. Contact service organizations that may be willing to collect lightly used books or buy books for the school and classroom libraries.
3. Contact community centers and religious, government, and service organizations to see if they will sponsor presentations about proposed changes. They provide the room and refreshments, and the school provides an employee or trained volunteer, and translator if appropriate, to make the presentation. This helps reach out to families and community members who may not have transportation or feel comfortable coming to the school.
4. Contact service organizations and youth organizations to provide game or food booths at school fundraisers, such as a Fall Festival.
5. Contact community organizations and media to see if they will announce upcoming school events in their calendar of events or newsletters. This may help reach family members and community members who do not see other announcements and serve as an extra reminder to other families. Keep a list of places that will post or announce events for free, such as local National Public Radio stations, so that each time there is an upcoming event, notices can be sent in advance.

References

Deslandes, R., & Rivard, M. C. (2013). A pilot study aiming to promote parents' understanding of learning assessments at the elementary level. *School Community Journal, 23*(2), 9–31.

Gaitan, C. D. (2004). *Involving Latino families in schools: Raising student achievement through home-school partnerships.* Thousand Oaks, CA: Corwin Press.

Hattie, J. (2012). *Visible learning for teachers: Maximizing impact on learning.* New York, NY: Routledge.

Hernandez, J. C., & Baker, A. (2013, April 19). A tough new test spurs protests and tears. *New York Times.* Retrieved from www.nytimes.com/2013/04/19/education/common-core-testing-spurs-outrage-and-protest-among-parents.html

Hernandez, J. C., & Gebeloff, R. (2013, August 7). Test scores sink as New York adopts tougher benchmarks. *New York Times*. Retrieved from www.nytimes.com/2013/08/08/nyregion/under-new-standards-students-see- sharp-decline-in-test-scores.html?pagewanted=1&_r=0

Minnich, C. (2014, March 27). Field testing Common Core assessments—A big step toward a worthy goal. *Huff Post Education*. Retrieved from www.huffingtonpost.com/chris-minnich/field-testing-common- core_b_5041854.html

Rubin, R., Abrego, M. H., & Sutterby, J. A. (2012). *Engaging the families of ELLs: Ideas, resources, and activities.* Larchmont, NY: Eye on Education.

Other Resources

Common Core information in English and Spanish. www.colorin colorado.org/common-core/parents/languages/

Common Core State Standards Initiative (2014). Preparing America's students for success. Retrieved from www.corestandards.org/

Ferlazzo, L., & Hammond, L. (2009). *Building parent engagement in schools.* Santa Barbara, CA: Linworth Books.

Marsh, M. M., & Turner-Vorbeck, T. (Eds.). (2010). *(Mis)understanding families: Learning from real families in our schools.* New York, NY: Teachers College Press.

PTA about Common Core. *Parents' guide to student success [English and Spanish].* Retrieved from http://pta.org/files/Common%20 Core%20State%20Standards%20Resources/2013 %20Guide%20 Bundle_082213.pdf

PTA about Common Core. *Parents' guide to student success [Vietnamese and Arabic].* Retrieved from www.louisianabelieves.com/ resources/library/family-support-toolbox-library

Ravitch, D. (2013, November 25). Why so many parents hate Common Core. *CNN Opinion*. Retrieved from www.cnn.com/2013/11/25/ opinion/ravitch-common-core-standards/

12

Overcoming Obstacles

To achieve results with excellence, you must focus on a few wildly important goals and set aside the merely important.

Steven Covey, 2013, p. 283

Scenario
Team Up for Change

Mr. Lopez had been a principal for eight years when he was selected in January to help open a new elementary school the following school year. The district had selected an interim principal for his former school so he could focus on getting ready for the new school.

He knew what obstacles he had faced at his former school and wanted to be proactive as much as possible at the new school. Mr. Lopez believed that hiring the best people possible was the most important component of setting up the new school. He knew that if he found good people and gave them the support they needed, his job would be much easier. He wanted to hire a good mix of seasoned and new teachers.

Mr. Lopez decided to give the candidates for teaching positions scenarios to help him learn more about how they would react in different situations. He was looking for teachers that valued working in teams and wanted continuous opportunities for growth. Mr. Lopez also wanted to see teacher candidates design and teach a lesson to real students. He planned to use a group of fourth-grade students in his former school's afterschool program for the teaching demonstration. Watching a demonstration lesson would allow Mr. Lopez to see how well the teacher engaged students in learning and see how well they met the learning expectations of the standards. After the lesson finished, he planned to also let the candidate reflect in writing about what he or she felt went well and what they would change if they taught the lesson again.

In addition to filling teacher positions, Mr. Lopez also had an opportunity to hire an assistant principal and dean of instruction. Mr. Lopez hoped to find candidates who were strong instructional leaders and had experience with instructional supervision strategies such as action research, book study groups, lesson study groups, peer coaching and/or professional learning communities. He had limited funds for professional development and hoped to promote ongoing learning opportunities for teachers throughout the regular school day. He also hoped that the assistant principal and dean of instruction would bring a strong background on assessing student learning through the use of a variety of formative assessments. His last dean was limited in his knowledge of student assessments and how to analyze data.

Mr. Lopez had someone in mind for the librarian position, Ms. Sanders. Ms. Sanders was an experienced librarian who had created a school media center well equipped with technology that supported student learning and curiosity. She was well known for helping students develop a love for research. Teachers also appreciated her willingness to help find materials for multi-disciplinary lessons. She led a technology committee at her school that worked hard to gather input from teachers about their needs. Mr. Lopez had also heard her speak at a district principals' meeting about ideas on how to increase the amount of informational texts for students. She was exactly what he needed. If Ms. Sanders was not available, he would keep looking until he found such a candidate.

Putting together the "dream team" at his new school was a challenge, but knowing the key areas to address would help him prevent or overcome many of the obstacles that were sure to arise. Change was never easy but with a strong team there would be a lot of support for students and teachers.

Change Is Difficult

Change is a difficult process and no matter how important or significant changes may be, they will encounter obstacles. We have tried here to describe a few of the obstacles that may be encountered as schools try to implement the *less is more* ideas, especially in light of Common Core and high-stakes testing. We then present ideas to counter these obstacles, but these are just suggestions, certainly not prescriptions for every school or every classroom. In fact, our focus is on providing the flexibility needed for educational leaders and teachers to discover and meet the needs of their students.

Most of our ideas do not require money at all, but there are some, such as upgrading technology, that will require schools, districts, states, and other funding entities to set technology as a high priority. Although some of our ideas require time, we have tried to find ways that educators can rethink the use of time so that their time is focused on what Covey (2013) calls the "wildly important," rather than simply adding on to educators' never-ending tasks. We also believe that it is important to acknowledge that there are other factors, such as childhood poverty, that significantly impact student learning, but are beyond the scope of this book.

Time for Deep Student Learning

Challenges

Throughout this book, we have argued that elementary school students need many opportunities for deeper learning throughout the curriculum. Educators already know how to achieve deeper learning. It can be achieved by having students read complete texts rather than short summaries or excerpts. It can be achieved by having students do research projects in which they ask questions, search for answers, analyze and summarize those answers, and share their findings with others. Educators know students need opportunities to view issues and problems from multiple perspectives rather than one simplified view.

Students need to understand problem-solving processes and apply them to a variety of problems, in math as well as other curriculum areas. They need to write narrative, informational, and persuasive texts with revisions and editing. Deeper learning also can be achieved by providing opportunities for students to work together on projects that encourage them to delve into topics and share their knowledge and viewpoints. Educators know all of this, but the problem is trying to find the time to get it done.

Ideas

In order to find this time, Sparks (2008) applied principles from Koch's 80/20 Principle to education. He wrote that educators should "identify the 20 percent activities that make the largest difference and spend more time in those activities" (p. 21). The first step in going in that direction is to identify the goals. Covey (2013) says that it is important to limit those goals because the fewer goals we have, the more likely we are to succeed in reaching those goals.

Once educators decide on their top goals, they need to determine if their classroom practices are supporting the goals. A great deal of research exists on effective and ineffective classroom practices. Recently, Hattie (2012) conducted a meta-analysis of more than 60,000 studies to determine the impact of various practices on student learning. For example, meta-cognitive programs, designed to help students become aware of their own thinking, have a high impact on student learning. On the other hand, practices such as teaching test-taking skills and individualized learning take a great deal of time and provide little effect. This type of goal setting and examination of classroom practices will help teachers spend more time on those things that have the greatest impact and less or no time on other practices.

In addition to reducing or eliminating the time spent on ineffective practices, educators can combine what they need to do so they can achieve more than one objective at a time through integrated units. One such unit might explore balance; balance in mathematical equations, balance in natural systems such as between predators and prey, checks and balances in government, and balance in art and architecture.

Time for Teacher Collaboration

Challenges

In order to achieve the goals of *less is more,* teachers need more time to collaborate in a culture of collegiality and professional learning. Teachers need time to decide on goals and plan integrated units. They need time to differentiate instruction for students with different needs, sometimes individually and sometimes with help from other educators. Teachers need to examine data from formative and summative student assessments to decide where to focus their time and energy. They need opportunities to observe one another and discuss their observations.

The implementation of Common Core standards and assessments make teacher collaboration even more important. The National Association of Elementary School Principals has compiled a checklist to help teachers and educational leaders assess their progress in implementing the Common Core, which is available on their website (in references). As changes are made, they need to discuss their successes and challenges. In short, teachers need time to learn from one another.

Ideas

Trying to find that time can be challenging, but there are a few ways that teachers can collaborate more without it costing schools more money or teachers more time. Just as teachers need to set priorities for student learning, educators need to set priorities for teachers' time as well. Which practices will have the greatest impact on student learning goals with the least output of money or additional time? For example, educational leaders can carefully examine the use of the current planning time, faculty meetings, and professional development. In many districts, money and time are expended on outside consultants, who are just at the school for a few days or less. These resources usually would have a greater impact if they were used for teachers to work on their high-priority goals together. Local consultants, online training, or other teachers could be used if a group of teachers felt they needed assistance in a specific area, such as integrating curriculum.

Most schools have once-a-week faculty meetings. Sometimes they may be needed to discuss school-wide goals or projects, but many faculty meetings could be replaced with e-mails, electronic surveys, and other less time-consuming means of communication. This time could then be used for well-structured, small group teacher collaboration sessions in which teachers work on predetermined goals, such as deciding how to differentiate instruction within a specific integrated unit, writing rubrics together to evaluate student writing, or examining data from formative assessments to help focus their instructional efforts.

In order to find time for teacher collaboration, observations, and conferencing, Gregory (2003) suggests having students from one grade level buddy with students from another grade level for paired reading or other activities once a week. Let's suppose that all fourth-grade classes are paired with all second-grade classes. Then all the second-grade teachers supervise all the students one week and all the fourth-grade teachers supervise the students the next week. This allows grade-level teachers to plan together and complete in-house professional development, and is especially valuable if it can be done before or after the teacher's regular planning period so that teachers have a block of time once every other week to work together. If grade-level teachers want to observe each other teaching, they can have a buddy plan but not all grade-level teachers participate at the same time so that while some are freed to observe, others are still teaching.

Need for Technology

Challenges

In this era, students need to be able to use computers, tablets, and the Internet fluently in order to succeed in higher education and life. At one time computers may have been considered a luxury, but that is no longer true; they are as important to education today as paper and pencil were 50 years ago. (The word *device* will be used here to indicate any learning device that allows students to access the Internet and to write digitally.)

Students need to have devices easily accessible to write, revise, and edit their work. No adult would dream of having to write a paper two or three times by hand in order to hone their craft, and no student should be expected to do so either. The Internet is a source of information that can provide multimedia information about a variety of topics that would cost far more if texts, videos, photographs, and educational games had to be purchased separately for the classroom and then repurchased as they are updated.

The Common Core requires that all elementary school students, even kindergartners, use "digital tools to produce and publish writing, including in collaboration with peers." From third grade on up, students are expected to use the Internet for research. In addition, the Common Core standardized assessments will be given on devices.

The federal government's ConnectED Initiative (2013) sets goals of having broadband connections and high-speed wireless for 99 percent of students by 2018. The initiative also calls for more professional development for teachers and educational leaders to best use technology to improve student learning. Unfortunately, many schools have a long way to go in terms of devices, professional development, and Internet connectivity. "Many schools are now seeing, late in the game, that the gap between what they have and what they need is troubling" (Bushweller, 2014, p. 7). He continues to explain that the State Educational Technology Directors Association reports that "72 percent of schools do not meet the basic Internet-bandwidth requirements . . ."

Throughout this book, we have promoted quality over quantity but when it comes to devices, quantity may be as or more important than quality. Device usage cannot be limited to a once a week trip to a computer lab or two computers in the back of the classroom. Nor can educators depend on students learning how to use devices at home.

Unfortunately, the cost of hardware and software are not the only challenges involved in integrating more technology into the curriculum. Teachers and educational leaders need to receive professional development on the best ways to use technology to promote a high-quality curriculum rather than allowing pre-packaged programs dictate the curriculum. Teachers also need ongoing technology support. They cannot be expected to take time away from teaching to solve technology problems. In addition, schools need to work out technology challenges, such as finding a balance between elementary students' access to inappropriate material and filters that block sites that they need for academic research.

Ideas

Devices and Internet connections need to meet the needs of assessments administered through devices. Beyond those necessities, teachers should have input on selecting technology to meet their curricular needs. For example, teachers may want to subscribe to websites that have materials appropriate for their grade level and integrated units. When teachers have input, technology is more likely to be used and integrated into the curriculum rather than being just another add-on that takes more classroom and teacher time as well as large sums of money.

In recognizing the need for more educational technology and related professional development, Culatta, director of the U.S. Department of Education's Office of Educational Technology, wrote an open letter (2014) to educators about using federal funds for technology related needs. He points out that "many federal formula and competitive grant programs allow funds to be used to support digital learning, even if the program statutes do not reference educational technology specifically" (para. 2). For example, Title I funds, especially at lower income schools, can go a long way toward purchasing devices if this is made a priority. Individuals with Disabilities Education Act (IDEA) funds can be used for technology that will support differentiation as identified in Individualized Education Programs (IEPs).

Districts also may be able to save money by providing higher-quality devices at testing grades and less expensive tablets or refurbished computers for the lower grades. Businesses might even be willing to donate devices that are still good but too slow for their needs for the lower grades.

Although there may be ways to reduce the cost of increasing technology in schools and apply federal funding for technology and related costs, there is no doubt that schools and districts will need to place a greater priority on funding the technology that is required for modern learning and assessments.

Students Need a Greater Variety of Texts

Challenges

Students need to read a variety of texts frequently in order to become critical readers and researchers. As part of the Common Core, students are expected to read more than one book on the same topic and, at the upper grades, read books that approach the same topic from different perspectives. There is also a greater emphasis on informational reading than many states had in the past. In order to differentiate instruction, the teacher must have access to books about the same topic at different reading levels. All of this translates into a great need for accurate, up-to-date, high-interest books in schools.

Ideas

With tight budgets, finding the money for books can be difficult. The following are ways that some schools are meeting the challenge. Although it would be ideal to have books on a wide variety of subjects, efforts first should be focused on the topics of the integrated units. In fact, one of the factors that teachers may want to use in choosing integrated units is what is available in textbooks and text sets already on the shelf. If you have multiple copies of one source on the topic, then this can be a starting point for the integrated unit, but other texts will still be needed. Calkins, Ehrenworth, and Lehman (2012, p. 94) also suggest planning "which of your units will be writing intensive, which will be media intensive, and which will be reading intensive. Then you will want to get an excess of nonfiction books on the topics within which you will especially emphasize nonfiction reading." Teachers in the same grade level also can stagger the time of year when they teach the integrated unit so resources can be shared.

Another way to find resources is to look through storerooms, warehouses, and even teachers' shelves for texts that are not being used. If there are old textbooks, try to find a volunteer to cut up the textbooks according to themes and use inexpensive bindings to make little books out of them. This is often a good way to have different leveled texts on hand. For example, an old second-grade social studies text might be cut up and used for different integrated units in second, third, and fourth grades. Just check to make sure that information is not outdated or expressing prejudicial views. If the sources are incomplete, they will most likely be supplemented with other sources on the topic anyway.

Texts do not always have to be books either. Many companies and non-profit organizations have brochures that they would be happy to donate to the school. Not only are these a good source of information, but they also can be used to help students understand different perspectives on the same topic. If the class is studying energy, natural gas companies may provide information about the advantages of natural gas fracking while an environmental group may share information on the disadvantages of natural gas fracking. If fracking is going on in the local area, this will be relevant to students. Fire and police departments, county health offices, agricultural extension services, nature centers, and tourist information centers all may have texts that could be used during an integrated unit, some of which are specifically targeted for young audiences. Local speakers also can augment the texts.

The Internet is another source of varied texts on topics. Although much of the information on the Internet is beyond an elementary school students' level, there are texts and videos designed for children. The Reading and Writing Project (www. readingandwritingproject.com) has lists of websites where teachers and students can find a variety of information representing different perspectives and difficulty levels on the same topic. Some examples are: pets in the classroom, bottled water, and wildfires. Webquests guide students through Internet research. Sites such as QuestGarden have multimedia integrated units that have been designed and used by other teachers and include multimedia resources on a variety of topics and levels.

Overemphasis on High-Stakes Testing

Challenges

Although it seems counterintuitive, more test preparation doesn't always result in better scores on the tests (Hattie, 2012). This was especially true with test preparation for most of the previous state assessments, which focused on low-level skills. "A growing number of parents and educators are uncomfortable with the fact that today's students are drilling for multiple-choice tests geared to the expectations of the past" (Darling-Hammond, 2014, p. 10).

The emphasis of the Common Core and other new state standards are on higher-order thinking skills, but no one assessment can assess the critical reading and research, problem solving, communication, collaboration, and independent work skills needed for today's world. In order to save time and money, high-stakes assessments focus on multiple-choice questions, which take less time to take and grade.

Too much test preparation often means that students miss out on the deep learning that can only be provided by spending extended time on one topic. When the focus of instruction is on preparing for tests, students don't have time to conduct research, read multiple perspectives on the same topic, work on solving complex problems, write and revise papers, collaborate, or work on projects. They don't develop extensive vocabulary because they are not exposed to the same words in a variety of contexts.

Drill and practice test preparation materials do not engage students either. Many may develop negative attitudes about school because they do not view the work as relevant or interesting. "Attitude plays a significant role in student performance, particularly at the lower grades" (Gulek, 2003, p. 44). In addition, test preparation programs fail to provide differentiation for the varied needs of students.

Ravitch, who was assistant secretary of education in the first Bush administration, once supported high-stakes, standardized testing to improve education and hold educators accountable for their students' performance. She now believes that the testing may be doing more harm than good. "And so we may find that we have obtained a paradoxical and terrible outcome: higher test scores and worse education" (Ravitch, 2010, p. 230).

Ideas

Most educators have little control over the high-stakes tests, but they usually have some influence over how they prepare students for the tests and how the scores on benchmarks and previous year's tests impact their treatment of individual students.

The Common Core and other state standards now emphasize the type of skills that will prepare students for higher education and careers. If teachers teach all of the standards rather than just the ones that they believe will be on the test, students will develop the thinking, communication, and collaboration skills that they need not only for the test but also for life. "When this is done, test scores will most likely take care of themselves" (Gulek, 2003, p. 43).

Benchmark assessments that measure students' progress against end of the year expectations do not provide teachers or students with the information they need to improve learning. Instead, formative assessment during the year should measure current learning goals and be designed to help teachers provide high-quality feedback to students and improve instruction quickly. Assessments, such as rubrics used for writing, projects, or presentations, also can be integrated into instruction and do not require extra time.

Even when teachers make sure that students are learning the standards and use formative assessments for student feedback and instructional improvement, they still need to take some steps to specifically prepare students for the tests. Students need to be familiar with the vocabulary and format of the tests, but this knowledge can be integrated into units rather than adding more to the day. For example, teachers can give tests at the end of integrated units that mirror the format of the high-stakes tests, such as multiple-choice and short-answer questions. As most states move toward computer-administered tests, it is also important that students become familiar with the use of computers for testing.

Finally, educators should use a wide variety of assessments to make instructional decisions for the class and individual students.

Teachers often look at test scores from previous years at the beginning of the new school year. Although this practice makes sense, teachers should remember that this is only one snapshot of a student's capabilities and they need to assess students many different ways to truly discover their strengths and needs.

Need for Flexibility

Challenges

Research indicates that teachers are the most important school-related influence on learning (Rand Corporation, 2012). Yet, many teachers, even excellent teachers, feel that they don't have the flexibility needed to maximize their students' learning.

Over the years, policy makers and others have tried to control what goes on in the classroom through teacher-proof curriculum. Some of this curriculum requires teachers to be on the same page at the same time; others actually have a script. The Common Core standards cannot be taught this way. "Teachers cannot push students to think more deeply unless they do so themselves" (Ruenzel, 2014, para. 5).

Even at schools without such rigid curriculum, teachers may be restrained by other factors. For example, students only can use computers or other devices for pre-programmed tasks. Scheduling is another limitation at some schools. Teaching may be departmentalized even at the elementary school level, which makes curriculum integration difficult. Pull-out programs also limit teachers' flexibility to teach integrated units to all their students. We know teachers who don't have all their students in the classroom except for a few minutes at the beginning and end of the day.

Ideas

Some policy makers argue that they must use highly structured curriculum because of ineffective teachers and the difficulty in removing them from schools. However, there is little evidence that rigid programs increase student learning. At the same time, these programs discourage effective and potentially effective teachers. Some continue teaching but no longer try to improve their instruction, while others leave the field entirely. Studies indicate that effective teachers will remain at schools where there is "an atmosphere of mutual respect and trust" (TNTP, 2012, p. 18).

At middle school and high school, departmentalization makes sense because the content of the learning is as important as the processes of the learning, but elementary school is laying the foundation for later subject area instruction. When instruction is departmentalized, teachers can't integrate instruction, they have less flexibility in their schedules, and students may not see the connections between different subject areas. Teachers do not get to know the students as well either. If teachers have particular talents, these can be capitalized on once or twice a week by teachers switching rooms within grade levels. For example, if a grade level is doing an integrated unit on light and energy, one grade-level teacher might do a lesson on light in art or photography for all the classes, another might do various science experiments with light, one might help students cook with solar energy, and yet another might read and have the students write poetry that includes references to light or energy. This way teachers' creativity would be unleashed, students would benefit from their passion and expertise, but students would still have one teacher for their integrated curriculum most of the time.

Finally, pull-out programs are a real challenge to flexible scheduling. The programs should be minimized as much as possible with teachers of special needs students providing as much support as possible for those students and their teachers within the mainstream classroom. When pull-out programs are necessary, as many students as possible should be pulled out at one time rather than staggering them throughout the day.

Change Is a Process

Challenges
Change cannot and should not happen overnight, but Americans are generally impatient; we want immediate results and when we don't get them, we move on to the next thing. No place is this more obvious than in the tenure of big city superintendents, which was 3.6 years in 2010 (Pascopella, 2011). This type of turnover

doesn't allow time for reforms to be implemented and the results assessed before a new superintendent comes in with new ideas.

This lack of continuity also results in many principals and teachers deciding that if they lay low, no one will notice that they are not really implementing the latest reform plan. They take a "this too shall pass" attitude.

Even when reforms are widely and reliably implemented, it may be many years before the results are evident in student achievement. Think about a fruit or nut tree. They may be growing and thriving, but it is often years before they produce fruit or nuts. Almond trees take two to four years to produce nuts, and sweet cherry trees take four to seven years to produce fruit. It would be a shame to cut down the tree because it didn't produce any fruit the first or second year, yet that is what happens with many educational reform programs.

Ideas

Educators need to convince themselves and others that effective change takes time. Although improvement in student learning and achievement is the ultimate goal, educational leaders and policy makers need to use formative assessments to evaluate, modify, and improve reform efforts. A variety of assessments should be used to determine the progress of implementation and challenges that are being encountered in order to respond to the needs of teachers and students.

Although it may take time, the *less is more* ideas of cutting, combining, and slowing down will ultimately help students, teachers, schools, and districts to focus on those things that are truly important for elementary school students' future education and careers.

Activities for Identifying and Overcoming Obstacles

Obstacle Assessment

Purpose: To help schools or districts to identify their greatest obstacles to improving instruction and possible remedies.

Participants: Anyone interested in improving education—students, teachers, educational leaders, families, and policy makers

The following are questions and notations that may help educators and others identify goals, obstacles, and possible solutions. This assessment would need to be conducted over several days or through multiple online interactions.

Activity Description

1. What is one extremely important goal for student learning?
    At the beginning, choose only one specific goal. As the school or district works to overcome the obstacles to that one goal, they may find that these same obstacles are blocking other goals. For example, a goal such as increasing students' higher-order thinking skills may also help with test scores and implementation of Common Core.
2. What are steps that should be taken to reach that goal?
    Brainstorm a list of all the things that would help the school or district to reach that goal. The tendency here is to say "yes, but . . . " The obstacles to the steps will be discussed later, but it is important to come up with as many ideas as possible to help achieve the goal. Additional ideas for almost any goal can be obtained free online.
3. Which of these ideas will have the greatest impact on student learning?
    Use experience and research to place the top ten ideas in order from greatest impact on student learning to least impact on student learning. Again, don't worry about obstacles right now.
4. What will be the approximate cost of each of the top ten ideas in terms of money, time, and personnel?
    These don't have to be exact costs, but each of the top ten ideas should have approximate costs in terms of money, additional time, or additional personnel.
5. Can other things be cut to implement these ideas?
    If this goal is truly the top priority of the school or district, then less important goals may need to be postponed or cut to reach this goal. For example, all professional development time and money could be focused on the goal for a year. Test preparation

materials that do not have a high impact on student learning could be replaced with materials that will help reach the goal.

6. What can be combined?

   Many schools are purchasing devices for computer-administered assessments. Can these same devices be used to help students reach the target goal? Can some of the ideas be combined to reduce the time or money required for them?

7. Could ideas be piloted with some students or teachers?

   Sometimes schools or districts do not want to spend the resources necessary to implement new ideas unless they know that they will work in their context. Perhaps some of the ideas to reach the goal could be tested with a relatively small number of students or teachers.

8. After considering what can be cut, combined, or piloted, which ideas are unrealistic?

   Reaching the goal should not require any educator to work more hours than would normally be expected without receiving additional compensation. *Less is more* focuses on cutting and combining to reach goals rather than just adding to the status quo. If ideas are still unrealistic, they should be removed from the list.

9. Choose the top three realistic ideas to reach the goal and develop a plan to implement them.

   The following are some of the questions that might be considered during the planning period.
   a) What materials are needed?
   b) What personnel will be involved?
   c) What will be the schedule for planning and implementation?
   d) Where will the funding come from?
   e) How will the plan be assessed? When?

Finding Resources

Purpose: To help schools and districts find the money, volunteers, and other resources needed to reach their goals.

Participants: Anyone who is willing to help

Federal Funding—Title I-Part A funds are designed to help children from low-income families and can be used for a variety of purposes including technology, books, and family engagement. Individuals with Disabilities Education Act (IDEA) funds can be used to assist disabled students in ways that are designated in their Individualized Education Programs (IEPs). Title II-A funds can be used for teacher and leader professional development.

Grants—If the district has a grant writer, he will be aware of many of the grants that are available. Educators and educational leaders should go through the proper channels to make sure the grant writer knows the priorities of the school or district. Not all grants are worthwhile. Some grants may require the school to move away from their priorities or may require so much time that there is little net benefit.

Fundraisers—www.fundraising-ideas.org offers a variety of fundraising ideas. Some are what they call "do it yourself" fundraising projects and others are through companies that specialize in fundraising projects for schools. They also offer advice about choosing projects that will work well in your community.

Service Organizations—Service organizations can help with gathering materials, such as books, and providing volunteers. There are adult service organizations associated with religious groups and other groups such as Lions and Elks Clubs. There are also service organizations for young people, such as Honor Societies and Boys and Girls Club. Rotary International partners with the International Reading Association to promote literacy.

Other Volunteers—Volunteers can help take pressure off the teacher. In addition to tutoring, volunteers can be used to put student work on bulletin boards or prepare copies and other materials, such as putting covers on student written books. Some school districts have volunteer coordinators who may be able to match volunteers with specific teachers and needs. Other sources of volunteers are college classes in which students are required to do relevant volunteer work, active retirement communities or organizations, or family members, including grandparents.

References

Bushweller, K. (2014). Digital advances, Common Core fuel new testing approaches: Technology and policy developments prompt a rethinking of assessment. *Education Week, 33*(25), 7–8.

Calkins, L., Ehrenworth, M., & Lehman, C. (2012). *Pathways to the Common Core: Accelerating achievement.* Portsmouth, NH: Heinemann.

ConnectED: President Obama's plan for connecting all schools to the digital age. (2013). Retrieved from www.whitehouse.gov/sites/default/files/docs/connected_fact_sheet.pdf

Covey, S.R. (2013). *The 8th habit: From effectiveness to greatness.* New York, NY: Free Press.

Culatta open letter to educators (2014, February). Retrieved from www.ed.gov/edblogs/technology/files/2013/06/Federal-Funds-Tech-DC-.pdf

Darling-Hammond, L. (2014). Testing to, and beyond the Common Core. *Principal, 93*(3), 8–12.

Gregory, G.H. (2003). *Differentiated instructional strategies in practice: Training, implementation, and supervision.* Thousand Oaks, CA: Corwin.

Gulek, C. (2003). Preparing for high-stakes testing. *Theory Into Practice, 42*(1), 42–50.

Hattie, J. (2012). *Visible learning for teachers: Maximizing impact on learning.* New York, NY: Routledge.

Koch, R. *The 80/20 principle: Detonating a time revolution.* Retrieved from www.thisbusinessforyou.com/pdf/The80–20Principleby RichardKoch.pdf

National Association of Elementary School Principals. Common Core Implementation Checklist. Retrieved from www.naesp.org/sites/default/files/common%20core%20checklist_2_22_2013as.pdf

Pascopella, A. (2011, April). Superintendent staying power. *District Administration.* Retrieved from www.districtadministration.com/article/superintendent-staying-power

Rand Corporation (2012, October). *Measuring teacher effectiveness: A resource for teachers, administrators, policymakers, and parents.* Retrieved from www.rand.org/topics/teacher-effectiveness.html

Ravitch, D. (2010). *The death and life of the great American school system: How testing and choice are undermining education.* New York, NY: Basic Books.

Ruenzel, D. (2014, March). Embracing teachers as critical thinkers. *Education Week.* Retrieved from www.edweek.org/ew/articles/ 2014/03/26/26ruenzel.h33.html?tkn=WSQFP %2FP4qPu9C5br%2 FPN3bcnsNBcDKmjfRhuF&intc=es&print=1

Sparks, D. (2008). Do less, achieve more. In V. von Frank (Ed.), *Finding TIME for Professional Learning* (p. 21). Oxford, OH: National Staff Development Council. (Original work published 2006).

TNTP. (2012). *The irreplaceables: Understanding the real retention crisis in America's urban schools.* Retrieved from http://educators 4excellence.s3.amazonaws.com/8/43/9/535/TNTP_Irreplaceables_ 2012.pdf

Other Resources

Donors Choose. www.donorschoose.org

Fundraisers www.fundraising-ideas.org

Jerald, C. (2010). Helping schools overcome barriers to change. The Center for Comprehensive School Reform and Improvement. Retrieved from www.education.com/reference/article/Ref_ Helping_School_Change/?page=2

Reading and Writing Project. www.readingandwritingproject.com

Rotary International. www.rotary.org/en/document/680

Webquest. http://questgarden.com/

13

Ten Keys to *Less Is More*

Education is not the filling of a pail, but the lighting of a fire.

William Butler Yeats

No one can predict the future or what careers will be available to someone who is now five-years old. Nevertheless, there are perennial skills that people will need regardless of what the future may bring. Reading with comprehension is vital whether the reading is done on papyrus or a screen. As the world becomes more complex, thinking and problem-solving skills increase in value. Clear communication is indispensable whether it is done through song, prose, or Twitter. People around the world are more connected than ever through technology, and thus, it is essential that we learn to collaborate with people who are different from ourselves. Since the future is unknown, we must have both the skills and the spirit to continue our learning throughout our lives.

Unfortunately, some have interpreted our ideas and those of the Common Core as a call to return to the basics of just reading, writing, and arithmetic. Nothing could be further from the truth. Although the basics are fundamental to all learning, they are not learned well in isolation from rich content. The Common Core and other state standards lend themselves to integrating learning in elementary school, where reading and writing may be done through drama, songs, history, or blogs. Problems may be investigated through mathematics, experimenting in science, or conducting research on current events. Although music, the arts, and movement may not be on most standardized tests, they have been shown to increase learning in almost every area, engage even reluctant students, and help differentiate instruction for the diverse needs of students in today's classrooms. Therefore, *less is more* is not about going back to the basics but rather covering less and learning more in a variety of ways. The following 10 points synthesize the important aspects of doing less, but doing it better.

1. Less Breadth and More Depth

Whether we are adults or children, we learn and remember things when we can make connections between the new information and previous experiences or learning. Isolated bits of information usually disappear from our memory quickly. When teachers spend weeks on one thematic unit, students are able to make these connections as well as practice their perennial skills.

Students cannot learn to brainstorm, write, and revise when only one or two hours are devoted to each writing project. They can't formulate questions, conduct research, and analyze and summarize the information found in a day or two. Even for short activities, such as an outside speaker, students will learn most when they are familiar with the topic in advance and have an opportunity to discuss the information presented after the speaker leaves in order to connect what the speaker said to their own knowledge and experience.

If teachers average one new integrated unit every four weeks, students will be engaged in nine different units per year. When teachers work together with others in their grade level, they can easily plan this number of units over a couple of years. If this model of thematic units was used throughout the elementary school years, each student would experience 54 different units.

2. Less Memorization and More Critical Thinking and Problem Solving

This is definitely the information age, where we can access a myriad of information day or night. Instead of memorizing information, more time needs to be spent on learning how to find the information students want and need, then evaluating the source and the information for validity and perspective. In addition to books, students receive information from television, Internet, radio, music, and other print sources. Students must become educated users of this information, questioning the purpose of the source and looking for conflicting information to help them draw their own conclusions.

Some simple problems may be quicker to solve if we can do addition, subtraction, multiplication, and division in our heads or memorize a formula, such as the Pythagorean Theorem, but that does not take us far in solving real-life problems. In life, solving a problem often requires multiple steps. Sometimes there are several possible solutions, which must be compared and evaluated to determine the best possible solution for the situation. Other times, there are no solutions, or at least not any good ones.

3. Fewer Worksheets and More Real Reading, Writing, and Problem Solving

Most worksheets help to focus students' attention on specific skills and offer practice on that skill in isolation. At times this is important but once students have a basic understanding of a skill they need to apply it during real reading, writing, and problem solving in order for students to remember and use the skill later. For example, a student may do well on a worksheet on suffixes but then have trouble figuring out the word "joyful" in their reading even though they can already read "joy." A student may do well on a worksheet on capitalizing proper nouns but forget to capitalize the names of places in their writing.

In addition, worksheets tend to focus on one skill at a time. When students have worksheets full of the same type of problems, such as word problems that require multiplication, they simply go through the worksheet happily multiplying. When they are suddenly faced with a variety of problems on a test or a problem that requires more than one mathematical operation, they are stuck because they have not learned how to analyze problems to determine a solution strategy from worksheets that focus only on one type of problem at a time.

4. Less Student Passivity and More Student Activity

This generation more than previous generations wants to be actively involved in their learning. Outside of class, they are figuring out computer or game programs. They are taking and finding photographs and sharing them with their friends. They download music and videos (legally and illegally). They are communicating with friends via social media. In direct contrast to this type of learning, most classrooms are dominated by teacher talk and individual student seatwork assigned by the teacher. Students are expected to receive information but have little opportunity to share their own ideas or choose what they learn or how they learn it.

In order to engage students in their learning, teachers should try to limit most of their direct instruction to mini-lessons in which they explain and demonstrate one important aspect of what they want students to learn. Students should have some choice about what they read, write, or research within the thematic units. They also should have options of how they demonstrate their learning. Just as students share a variety of information outside of school, they also should have many opportunities to share ideas with other students and the teacher within school. If educators want students to become lifelong independent learners, then they need to be empowered in elementary school to take some control and responsibility for their own learning.

5. Less Grading and More Effective Feedback

In addition to teaching all day, most elementary school teachers spend a great deal of their time in the evening and on weekends planning and grading because they want to spend their classroom time teaching. Unfortunately, educators are learning that much of the time they spend grading is probably wasted in terms of increasing student learning and achievement. Students often don't use their grades or even comments on their papers to improve their work.

Instead teachers should act more like athletic coaches, asking questions and prompting students to improve their work while they are working rather than giving them grades after the fact. This can be achieved by conferencing with individual students about their reading, writing, and problem solving. If students are working individually or in groups, the teacher can pull students aside to ask them questions about what they are reading or about how they can improve their writing or their problem-solving strategies. Although the teacher may not be able to conference with each student every day, they should be able to meet with each one a few times a week. When more grades are needed for report cards and other purposes, teachers can take a grade during these conferences or during student presentations. When papers are graded in more traditional ways, students should have an opportunity to discuss their mistakes so they are more likely to learn from them. If the assignment involved writing or showing work during a problem-solving activity, they should be given opportunities to redo the work and improve their grade to help them learn from their errors.

6. Less High-Stakes Test Preparation and More Formative Assessment

Although administrators and teachers usually have no control over end of the year high-stakes tests, they do have control over the way that students are prepared for those tests. Students need practice with the vocabulary and the format of the test, and, as testing moves to computers, students will need appropriate computer experience. However, none of this means that students should be submitted to a daily diet of test preparation materials at the expense of real reading, writing, and problem solving. Benchmark tests should measure what students have already learned rather than end of the year expectations.

Most assessment during the year should be formative assessment that is conducted during instruction to provide information for student coaching and feedback. This type of assessment also provides the teachers with information about concepts that have been mastered or those that require review or reteaching. When teachers regularly learn about students' progress toward their grade-level standards, they can adjust instruction to prepare students for high-stakes tests while still engaging students in authentic instruction and learning.

7. Less Teaching to the Middle and More Differentiation

In education, one size definitely doesn't fit all. Students differ in interests, abilities in different areas, English language proficiency, and emotional and social needs. One student may shine in mathematics while another shows perspective in their drawings in first grade. Some students may excel academically but need to develop their social and collaboration skills. Teaching for the average student in the class doesn't provide the differentiation needed for maximum student achievement.

Students learn the most when they are challenged but not frustrated. Although it may be difficult for all students to be at their own level all day long, students need to feel the joy that comes from accomplishing something that was previously challenging for them. All students can be involved in studying the same thematic unit but learning about the topics with different materials and modalities. The expectations and manner in which they show their knowledge and skills may also vary among students so that each can feel success rather than boredom or frustration.

8. Less Isolation and More Collaboration

More collaboration means more cooperation among students, among all school personnel, and among school personnel, families, and community members. Whether we are young or old, isolation limits us while collaboration expands the possibilities. What seems impossible alone becomes possible in a group.

Although collaboration often takes more time, the benefits are enormous. Collaboration gives us new ideas, more people to split the work, and more understanding of differing views. When we are trying to implement changes, there is likely to be less opposition if all interested parties are a part of the process from the beginning. After initial discussion, work may be divided to lighten the load, but interested parties should communicate regularly, especially as questions or challenges arise.

9. Fewer Directives and More Communication

Directives are instructions that only flow one way—usually from the teacher to the students, from the administrators to the teachers, or from the school to families and the community. Communication on the other hand involves information that flows both ways with flexible content and presentation that is modified as the oral or written communication continues. It is important, especially for those in positions of power, to listen as much or more than they speak or write. People not only want someone to listen to them but they also want to know that they are heard. If a student asks for help with something and the teacher promises to provide that help later, he must make sure that either he or someone else assists the student. If a parent complains to an administrator about something that is outside of his knowledge, such as an incident on the bus, the administrator must follow-up and contact the parent with that information.

There are many times when families or community members make requests that cannot be accommodated, such as changing the dates of state exams, but if they understand that someone has listened to their request and explained the reasons for the decisions, they will usually be satisfied. Even if teachers and administrators cannot do everything that is requested, they can improve relations and create climates of trust by listening and communicating rather than just giving directives.

10. Less Speed and More Thought

We want faster computers, faster phones, and faster meals. As we push for more speed in our lives and those of our students, we might step back and remember the old adage, "Haste makes waste." In many subtle and not so subtle ways, teachers often emphasize the speed and quantity of work completed rather than the quality and depth of work. For example, students might only be able to use the computers in the back of the room when they finish their work so some students will rush through their work in order to use a computer. At other times, teachers rush to finish a lesson before lunch or the end of the day when they could just as easily continue it after lunch or the next day to make sure that students have time to process the meaning(s) of the lesson. By reducing the breadth of what is taught to students, teachers can spend more time on each concept. Think of the difference between a fast food restaurant and a meal at a fine restaurant. Sometimes speed may be important, but students also need many opportunities to savor their learning.

Less speed and more thought also applies at the school, district, and community level. When teachers are forced to make changes too quickly, they often resist the efforts because they do not have time to personalize the changes and incorporate them into their own teaching style. On the other hand, when they are allowed to implement change slowly, they can see what works and what doesn't for them and make necessary accommodations for their students and themselves.

Districts that are about to make changes also need to take their time. Students, parents, teachers, administrators, staff members, and others should have opportunities for authentic participation in the decision-making process. Changes may be tested on a small scale before being implemented district-wide just as medicine goes through trial testing before it is sold to the general public. Policy makers need to consider all the possible "side-effects" and whether the benefits outweigh those side-effects before implementing change. For example, students need to learn to do Internet research for the Common Core, but schools also need to ensure that students are not exposed to inappropriate content or cyber bullying.

True learning and change takes time, thought, and flexibility. Students learn at different rates and in different ways. Students need time to discover their strengths and learning needs. Teachers need time to help each student make those discoveries and work on their needs. Schools and districts need time to make decisions, implement change, and evaluate change. At each level, it is important to be flexible so that modifications can be made that will best serve the needs of students.

Schools can't continue to add more and more to the curriculum and expect learning and achievement to improve. By cutting, combining, and slowing down, they can do less but do it better. This will ultimately result in a better school and community educational climate and students who learn more while becoming independent, lifelong learners.

Made in the USA
Coppell, TX
22 August 2022